P9-DDR-421

TRADING RULES

STRATEGIES FOR SUCCESS

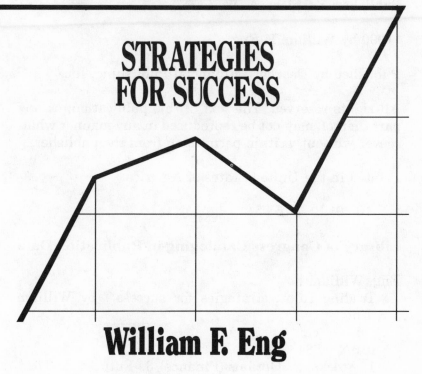

William F. Eng

Dearborn
Financial Publishing, Inc.

While a great deal of care has been taken to provide accurate and current information, the ideas, suggestions, general principles and conclusions presented in this book are subject to local, state and federal laws and regulations, court cases and any revisions of same. The reader is thus urged to consult legal counsel regarding any points of law —this publication should not be used as a substitute for competent legal advice.

Publisher: Kathleen A. Welton

©1990 by William F. Eng

Published by Dearborn Financial Publishing, Inc.

All rights reserved. The text of this publication, or any part thereof, may not be reproduced in any manner whatsoever without written permission from the publisher.

Printed in the United States of America

   10 9 8 7 6 5

Library of Congress Cataloging-in-Publication Data

Eng, William F.
   Trading rules: strategies for success / by William F. Eng.
      p.   cm.
   ISBN 0-88462-920-1
   1. Stocks. 2. Options (Finance) 3. Futures. I. Title.

HG4521.E583   1990
332.64—dc20   89-14593
                                                    CIP

DEDICATION

I wish to dedicate this book to two people.
My son, Alden, who just turned one year of age.
And to a special trader who passed away years ago.
As there is life, there is death.
When one cycle ends, another begins.

ACKNOWLEDGMENTS

I wish to thank Tim Slater, of Computrac, for the use of the output of Version 2.8 to illustrate parts of this book. Similar thanks go to William Forsyth and Steven Achelis, of Equis International, for use of the MetaStock Professional output to illustrate other parts. Thanks go to Jack Hutson, publisher of *Stocks and Commodities* magazine, for the use of the liquidity data chart.

Thanks to all my students who have expressed interest in becoming more proficient traders. Their questions and weaknesses showed me what my weaknesses as an educator were. I hope the knowledge that they gain from my writings and trading philosophies enriches their lives. The fact that they can make money in the markets will make them more helpful to others who are less talented. Not everyone wants to be a trader; yet everyone needs help—sometime, somewhere.

And final thanks to all the market analysts who have gone before me. Without their knowledge and techniques, the writing of this book would have been difficult, if not impossible.

Views expressed in this publication are solely those of the author and are not to be construed as the views of the Chicago Board of Trade, nor is the Chicago Board of Trade in any way responsible for the contents thereof.

CONTENTS

Contents

Contents

INTRODUCTION

One morning in the summer of 1982 I was eating breakfast in the Chicago Board of Trade's lower level dining room when I saw David Goldberg, a partner at Goldberg Brothers. David and his brother, Robert, who later became chairman of the Chicago Board of Trade, presciently saw the growth of options trading. They emphasized clearing operations in the developing markets. Equity options began trading in 1973 at the Chicago Board Options Exchange. Since that time, the Goldberg clearing operation had been one of the top five clearing firms.

David was sitting alone, so I walked over with my tray of food and asked if I could join him for breakfast. He looked startled, for he had been deep in thought, but he invited me to sit down. We discussed briefly how things were going, and then he changed the subject and began talking about how long it took to be a successful trader at the Chicago Board of Trade.

"It's so tough for a trader to get into the business now. A young guy has to come in with $100,000 to cover his first three years of trading." Then he glanced at his watch, guzzled the last drops of his black coffee, and said, "I have to go, Bill. Bonds opened half an hour ago. I've got to talk to Bill Cousins." He pushed his chair back and walked briskly out of the cafeteria.

I sat there looking at the space that David had just occupied. I had managed to take some time from his life and got valuable nuggets of information. Cousins was the margin clerk for Goldberg clearing operations. He was responsible for watching the traders' positions and for checking the daily runs. When he had to, he physically yanked traders out of the pit and liquidated their positions. At times like these, traders lost control of their accounts. They froze in the pits as their equity eroded rapidly. One day they have several thousand dollars in their accounts and the next day they owe the clearing firm money.

For the rest of the day I watched the bonds move up. They finally bottomed after moving away from the secondary bottom created several weeks earlier. This upside move was in earnest. The five year bear market had ended. Over the years I had trained myself to follow major trends. I realized that the bonds made a secondary bottom and removed myself from the bond pit. When markets end a long trending, one-directional move, I always found myself continuing to trade in the direction of the previous trend. In my own trading I always lost money when the markets bottomed or topped out.

I was not the only one to trade like this. I wondered who in the pit was still trading against this bond upmove. A week earlier Ricky "the Rocket" Barnes had bought the bottom. The traders he bought from either covered their shorts by buying them in at higher prices, or else were completely out of the game. I had sold some at the bottom, but I covered them when the market went up afterwards. Another trader was not so fortunate. He sold 200 bonds at the bottom and then got nailed by the ensuing violent upswing.

Two days after my breakfast talk with David Goldberg, I was sitting in the traders' lounge at the Trans Union building. The markets were quiet, and we all sat there checking the Quotron machines for price movements. Suddenly a trader from the options floor came up to me and asked if I had heard what happened to Larry

Thomas. I shrugged my shoulders and said, "No, I haven't talked to him for about a week. I've got to call him though. We're trying to get a deck together to handle the new bean options that are going to trade soon. We plan to make some solid money." The trader looked at me and asked, "Didn't you hear? He committed suicide. He shot himself in the head Sunday."

Stunned, I looked at the trader. I looked but did not see. I breathed but did not exhale. The trader explained that Larry Thomas had sold bonds short Friday morning; then the bonds went up and he sold more. He lost between $50,000 and $70,000 before the day was over. Despondent over his trading losses, he drank heavily that weekend. He called his parents and argued with them. He discovered that he did not love his girlfriend. His childhood frustrations cropped up. With the mounting pressure to succeed in trading, in relationships, in life, he broke. He put the muzzle of his gun to his mouth and pulled the trigger Sunday night.

Even as I write this book six years later, I still feel the loss of a close friend.

The week before his death, Larry and I had talked about the bonds. I told him to be careful about trading on the bear side. He called me "Professor." Over the years I taught him how to count the waves in the Elliott wave theory. I taught him Gann analysis. He was an eager student and he learned well. I taught him technical analysis, yet my message failed to enter his mind.

Death is a fact of life. Over the years I have befriended traders who committed suicide over losses caused by market action. I can remember the names and faces of four traders who ended their lives in such desolation. Larry Thomas was someone special to me. I saw in him my own life at the start of my trading career. He struggled to make money, just as I did when I started. I saw him search for knowledge, as I did when I failed in trading. I saw the successful trading techniques come to fruition for him, as they did for me when I traded the markets correctly.

What Larry Thomas did was exceptional. He lacked that one quality that all successful traders must have. He lacked hope.

With hope you can overcome obstacles. With hope you can do all the things you thought you could not do. With hope the worst losers can ride the biggest bull markets. With hope, Larry could have succeeded in whatever he considered important in his life. With hope, he could even have come back from failure.

Hope alone, however, does not guarantee success. Hope coupled with knowledge of trading techniques and discipline will make you a winner in the markets.

I've compiled a list of 50 trading rules and thoughts that I consider the best I have seen over the years. I have illustrated each trading rule with examples that will help you recognize situations where you can use the rules. However, you must use caution when applying these rules. Indiscriminate application of rules, regardless of market stages, is very dangerous. It is akin to driving a car in a three dimensional world with one eye shut. You'll be all over the place, with no clear sense of where you want to go.

With the information from this book you will be on the road to market knowledge. With that knowledge you can trade successfully for the rest of your lives. Without it, you might as well go into another business.

Good luck in your trading. Remember, it's only a game.

"Would you tell me, please, which way I ought to go from here?" said Alice to the rabbit.

"That depends a good deal on where you want to get to," replied the rabbit to Alice.

—Lewis Carroll, *Alice in Wonderland*

RULE 1

Divide Your Trading Capital into Ten Equal Risk Segments

This rule of money management is widely credited to William D. Gann, the author and trader who developed innovative trading methods in the early part of this century. I have monitored my own trading results and modified this approach to equity management even further. If you follow my approach, you will never run out of trading capital, no matter how badly you trade.

Let's think about this rule and the situation surrounding it. You open a trading account with a finite amount of capital. With this capital you wish to take risks and make more money. In essence, what you are doing is putting your money into the market, a pool of funds, and acquiring an interest in it. If someone is willing to pay you more for your interest in the markets, then you sell your interests for a profit. It's as simple as that.

When you start to trade the markets, you should enter trades as if you expect to win on every one. It's important to have confidence in the success of your trades. If you don't, you will never trade risky positions, and those are the ones that have the greatest potential for profits. Nonetheless, you can't realistically expect that each trade will turn into a winner. The markets have many ways to make you lose money.

The only real winner in the market in the long term is the market itself. But individual traders are finite and must view the markets in shorter terms. It is in the shorter term that individual traders can profit. The problem with random walk theorists is they have no clear definition of time perspectives. They claim that there is no need to analyze the markets because all market movements are random. The purchase of any stock will give an average return over the life of the holdings.

The saying, "Take time out from trading. You can always go back to it," implies that the markets will always be there. An undisciplined trader who trades even in bad times offers the market the opportunity to outlive his or her trading equity.

As an individual trader you are finite and you have finite trading equity. The market, on the other hand, is a conglomeration of many traders and has infinite resources. It can match you dollar for dollar. If you lost a dollar and the market lost a dollar, it would still have the superior position.

If you think of the trading game as one in which you are trading against the market, you will see what I mean. If you make a dollar, somebody in the market lost a dollar. If the markets are now worth a trillion dollars, you cannot accumulate all the profits of the market valuation in your lifetime. Not so with what you can lose. You can lose a dollar and the market will suck it up and demand more. You can lose all your trading equity, and the market will meander about looking for more equity from traders like yourself. In short, you can probably win a finite amount of money from the market, but you can definitely lose all that you have. It makes sense to limit your exposure to market losses.

The problem rests with how much exposure of trading equity you should risk. How much money are you willing to let the market take away from you before you take your money and put it elsewhere? From my experience in the futures market, the maximum amount that I feel comfortable risking is no more than 2.5 percent of my total trading capital on any one position. Some of you may laugh at this extremely conservative number.

The maximum to risk on any one trade is the recommended 10 percent. Anything more than that will mathematically affect your ability to survive even a modest string of losses. If you risk a flat rate of 10 percent of your initial trading capital, you will have a 1/64 chance of losing all ten trades. One chance in 64 of ten straight losing trades is low. With this probability you should be able to get a winner somewhere in the string of ten trades. Then the question gets down to whether the amount won on the winners is enough to offset the losses on the losers.

I have modified the flat 10 percent of total starting capital to be a percentage of the remaining balance in your trading account. In this way, there will never be a zero balance in your account. To carry out this strategy, you need merely take a percentage of your remaining balance as the amount risked on each trade.

There are two distinctly different ways of measuring winners. I make a distinction between winning trades and dollar amount won on the winners. In the course of making a trade, if the position shows a tick profit, most people would consider this a winner. Technically, it is a winner, but you will need a series of these to be able to make a substantial profit. I would rather trade a minimum one lot and squeeze the trade for many ticks before I consider the trade a winner. This is being harder on myself because I must not only initiate a trade that shows a minimum one tick profit, but also generate many more tick profits before I can consider it a winner.

Another point enters into the rationing of risk positions and exposing your capital to risk. If you went to Las Vegas and played the roulette wheel, you would find that in the long run you would wind up losing money. That's because of the 36 numbers that you can bet on, 17 are black and 17 are red. There are two numbers that belong to the house. With two to the house, you have slightly less than an even chance of winning if you just bet on the colors. If the house removed the two extra numbers so that you had exactly a 50 percent chance of winning when betting on colors only, your long-term chances would have improved dramatically. Would you play the game under such conditions?

The foolhardy gambler would rationalize that he now has the same chances of winning that the house has: an even chance. The smart gambler, however, would recognize the very subtle difference derived from the odds, which are not shown in the mere probabilities of the roulette wheel. This subtle difference is based on the theory of runs. Let's assume that you had a capital base of $10,000 to play the roulette wheel. At perfectly even odds you would still be at a disadvantage based on the amount of capital that the house has at its disposal. If the house has a capital base of $10,000,000 to play against you, you would find that eventually you would lose your $10,000. If you experienced a run of bad trades, you could lose all your betting capital of $10,000, and you would be out of the game. If the house loses $10,000 first to you, your capital would have doubled from $10,000 to $20,000. The house still has $9,990,000 left. What I am talking about here is a streak of losses. With $10,000,000 of capital at the house's disposal it can stand a series of 1,000 losses of $10,000. If you have one streak of a $10,000 loss, you are out of the game.

4

You must divide your risk capital into equal risk segments of 10 percent or less, preferably a defined percentage of declining equity balance. Then you must push the odds of successful trading to better than 50 percent in your favor. Just to obtain even odds will cause you to lose money in the end.

R U L E 2

Use a Two-Step Order Process

Thomas Temple Hoyne published a book in 1922 titled *Speculation: Its Sound Principles and Rules for Its Practice.* Imagine my surprise when he mentioned this trading strategy, which I developed for myself with my own resources. When he placed an order to enter a market, he also entered a stop loss order at the same time. He called this his two-order rule. The fact that someone else already thought of this trading strategy before me only serves to validate it. *Certain trading techniques and approaches span all markets through all time.* They have obvious applications in profitable trading strategies.

Losses will take you out of the market faster than a margin clerk. Profits won't. From this standpoint alone, it is critical that you provide some mechanism in your trading that will prevent your losses from becoming insurmountable. I use stop loss orders to prevent total erosion of my trading capital.

Stop loss orders are entered with your broker. The broker executes them when the market price moves to that level. The stop sell order is executed when the price reaches down and hits your stop price; the broker sells out your position. If the price reaches up to your stop buy price, the broker is obligated to buy in your position. You must make a distinction between a stop loss order and a stop loss *limit* order. In the case of a simple stop loss order, once the price on your limit is reached, the order is executed at the prevailing market price. With the stop loss limit order, once the price of your limit is reached, the order is executed at the price that is specified on the order. The problem with this type of order is that the actual market may have moved away from the limit price so your order may not actually be executable. Different exchanges accept different types of stop orders. You must check with your exchange and your broker to see if they will accept the orders that you want to enter.

My personal feeling is to use stop orders that are triggered when the limit is reached and executed at the prevailing market price. The object of the stop order is to limit losses because of bad market judgment. If the price of the item you are trading is going against you, you have to get out at any cost. Don't play for price at this point; play for position: The original pricing of your position is obviously wrong, so get out of it. Get back in later at a better price.

Most traders use stop loss limit orders to close out opposite positions. If they are short, they enter a stop buy order to prevent the price from reaching higher and damaging their equity further. The converse is true with long positions. They use stop sell orders to prevent erosion of their capital.

Some experienced traders use stop limit orders to initiate positions instead of closing them out. These orders are often placed outside of trading ranges. When the orders are executed, the traders expect a continuation in the direction of the breakout of the trading range. For example, if a stock has been trading between $5 and $10 for several months, the experienced trader enters a stop limit buy order at $10.25. This order is executed when the stock trades above the $10 level and touches $10.25. The trader speculates on the strength of the stock. If the price of the stock has enough power to break through the trading range to the upside, it is showing enough strength to continue beyond $10.25.

The conventional wisdom concerning stop loss orders centers around using price as the triggering number. This is not always the case. Some traders use time as the trigger for liquidating positions. The Market Profile® technique developed and made popular by Peter Steidlmayer uses the passage of time as the limiting factor. If one were to trade using the Market Profile® technique, one would expect some major occurrence to happen within the confines of the trading day. If this expected occurrence does not happen within a certain time frame, the position is closed out no matter where the price is at.

Financial astrologers, the esoteric market traders, use time as an entry and exit factor. At certain times of the day or week they will enter positions because their trading techniques call for market entry.

So we have seen the application of stop loss orders as defined by either price or time. There are also rare cases where stop loss orders can be defined by trading volume. In fact, the only viable technique for tracking market activity through volume is the one developed by Joseph Granville—On-Balance Volume (OBV). On-Balance Volume, in a simple sense, is a cumulation of up volume versus down volume on a particular stock or futures contract. Over time, the cumulation forms a trending zigzag-shaped chart. When the OBV shows accumulation, independent of what the price at that particular coincid-

---

Market Profile® is a registered trademark of the Chicago Board of Trade, which holds exclusive rights to the Market Profile® graphics.

ing time is, OBV practitioners can use the upside volume breakouts as buy indicators and enter the market using this as the signal. There is a problem with using OBV breakout points as a type of stop loss order because they do not offer enough time to liquidate positions. Hence, the OBV technique is effective only on the buy side.

We have discussed the use of stops as a critical factor in market success. Some investors might counter and say that they have placed stops, which were then executed, only to see the market resume in the other direction. This, unfortunately, reinforces their original decision to enter the market on the right side. After the slight retracement, which was enough to catch their stop, they have no position in a correctly analyzed market. If you think about why you use stops—to limit losses on bad trades—you will realize that your stop was triggered because price went against your position, not because your position was bad.

The real problem is where to place the stops. Remember that the viability of the two-order rule is not invalidated by market movements that take you out of a winning position. What this means is that you don't know where to place the stops correctly.

Let's look at one extreme case of stop placement. Several years ago, when I was a broker with a small brokerage firm, I had a client who was a hog producer. He needed to use the futures markets to hedge the price of his hogs. The markets were bullish, and as long as they went up he didn't really need to sell any of his hog production. We decided to place a trailing stop and follow the markets up. This allowed the markets to stop him out into a long cash hogs/short futures hogs hedge when it topped out. Even here we weren't sure where to place the trailing stop. Do we place it 10 percent below the previous market close, after a major key reversal day, or use one of the countless other approaches that were then available?

I settled on something very basic for sheer lack of any definitive number to use as a limit. Every day we ratcheted the stop loss order up to a fraction of a cent above a limit down move. Futures contracts in the United States have limit moves. In past hog markets, when the price reversed from a sustained one directional move, it went limit. Therefore, if the hogs had enough weakness to sell off the first time, I wanted to have the hogs hedged right then and there. Well, the first time the market broke, it did go limit down, and we were hedged perfectly. In a purely mechanical way we hedged our cash production and used a minimum of market analysis.

The above anecdote illustrates one simple fact of using stop loss orders: Regardless of what you think about your market, you must have a stop loss order somewhere. It can be 10 percent of market price or whatever number you want. It might even be as ridiculous as half of current market price! I have seen enough market moves to know that even the ridiculous becomes patently sound given the right market conditions. Had you used a simple 25 percent of last previous price prior to the stock market meltdown of October 1987, you would have retained a good portion of your profits.

R U L E 3

Don't Overtrade

Overtrading was a problem that took me a long time to overcome because I didn't know what I was looking for. Let me recount a story about a trader at the Chicago Board of Trade that illustrates how serious a problem veteran traders regard overtrading to be.

A second generation floor trader had DOT as his badge acronym although those letters were not the initials of his name, William Jones. While trading in the Major Market Index (MAXI) pit one day, I heard the trader's father say "And remember, don't overtrade." That's what DOT meant: Don't overtrade! I thought it was a clever idea to incorporate a trading rule into an acronym. Little did I know that this brief trading rule would be critical to my own survival in the pits.

If you have been trading for a long time, you know that overtrading is a ubiquitous problem. And if you have ever tapped out of the trading profession, the chances are that you got yourself into trouble by overtrading. You lost more money than you had in your account.

When I was trading full time, I took naps in the clearing firm's lounge. One particularly grueling morning I dozed off in a couch next to Robert Goldberg's office. Robert was a partner in the Goldberg Brothers company. When I awoke I overheard him call a phone clerk on the bond floor and give an order to sell five contracts. I found it strange that a partner in a multimillion dollar clearing operation would be trading a mere five lot.

Four years later I was in the MAXI pit trading my usual twos and threes. Peter Steidlmayer, developer of the Market Profile® trading technique, walked into the pit and offered a one lot, then another one. He sold a total of five contracts and walked away from the pit. Later in the day the market moved against his position, so he came back into the pit and bought five contracts back. I sold him a couple contracts and, as I was carding the trade, he told me that he had to close out all his trades. The total commitment to his analysis was five short contracts, and he bought them all in. I was puzzled at the small size these two extremely well-capitalized traders initiated, but I later found out that it's not the size of your trades, but how you trade your winners and losers. I have heard the statement, "Size kills," often in the pits. These two traders knew what this meant.

Let me explain what overtrading means and how you can get into trouble by not knowing that you're overtrading.

You can buy low priced items for cash, but when the items get higher priced, the sellers make them more attractive to a cash-poor buying public by offering payment programs and credit terms. This means that you can buy a high priced item for a fraction of its total cost and then make payments on it until the balance is paid off. People buy food on a cash basis and they buy high priced items like cars and real estate on a credit basis.

Since there is no basic need to buy stocks or futures as there is to buy clothing, food, or shelter, sellers of stocks or futures offer "credit" terms as an inducement to prospective buyers. You can buy any number of stocks or futures by merely putting a small percentage of the total purchase price in your trading account. In stocks, this small percentage is called margin money. In futures, it is called a "good faith" deposit. In both cases, the money you use to control 100 percent of the stocks or futures is a small percentage of the total purchase price. The balance is to be paid off on demand.

This evolved into leverage, whereby a small amount of capital can be used to control a larger piece of assets. For stocks, margin has run from a low of 5 percent to as high as 75 percent. So from a low of $5 to a high of $75, you could control $100 worth of stocks. When the $100 worth of stocks gains $10 in value to a total market value of $110, the full cash buyer would receive a 10 percent return. The margin buyer who makes an investment of $5 would make $10 in this particular situation, or a 200 percent return. If margin is 75 percent, then $75 is required to control $100 worth of stock. A $10 return on a $75 investment amounts to a 13.33 percent return. Hence, you can see how margin benefits the investor.

In the futures markets, there are no margin requirements. Instead, the industry works with good faith deposits, which speculators must have at all times in their trading account. The deposits range from 3 percent to 10 percent of the actual market value of the futures contract. For all practical purposes, the deposits are similar in function to margin: They allow you to control more assets that you could buy outright.

Leverage also works against investors or speculators when the price of the investment or speculation goes against them. I've illustrated how an appreciating price multiplies the returns. If the price of the asset deteriorates, a cash buyer loses a percentage of the full $100. A loss of $5 means a 5 percent loss. A loss of $10 means a loss of 10 percent. The margin buyer encounters fast dete-

15

rioration of capital when the price of the asset drops. The 10 percent margin buyer would only have to put up $10 to control $100 worth of stocks. If the stock drops from $100 to $95, which is a 5 percent loss of the original market value, the margin buyer at 10 percent would suffer a 50 percent loss of his or her $10 investment. A $10 loss would mean a full 100 percent loss of the investment. If the price drops $15, from $100 to $85, the cash buyer would sustain a 15 percent loss; the margin buyer at 10 percent would sustain the full loss of the $10 margin money, and an additional $5. Such is the way margin, or good faith deposit, works. This little exercise in the mechanics of margins and good faith deposits is not without reason. One of the dangers of trading has always been overtrading. The business of trading is to make the stocks or futures reasonably priced so more people can invest and speculate. You can expect that margin and good faith deposits are used extensively in the business.

Let's move on to futures contracts to continue the discussion. Good faith deposits are calculated with a basic formula: Bring in the greatest number of market participants without getting them too highly leveraged. The greater the number of traders and players in the futures markets, the more money the exchanges make through sales of data, commissions, and transaction fees. Even though exchanges are set up as nonprofit organizations, they continue to survive and thrive. When prices are low, the margins are low. There is less daily volatility, so a minimum amount will cover the volatility. In such situations, there are fewer market players, so there is no need to worry about the players not having enough money to cover market losses.

When prices get high, the exchanges and clearing firms increase the good faith deposits to weed out the undercapitalized traders. It also protects the trader's account from getting wiped out by daily price volatility.

R U L E 4

Never Let a Profit
Turn into a Loss

This is a simple enough rule that everybody applies
without thinking about. When a floor trader first told me
about it I dismissed him as being overly cautious. I continued to make the mistake of selling out my winners and
keeping my losers. As a young trader, my mistakes could
be overcome; as I get older, the mistakes are more difficult to overcome.

Let's go through the process of placing a trade to illustrate how I manage to maintain a profit in it. When I
make a decision to buy or sell a futures or a stock, I also
figure out how much I am willing to risk on the trade.

Let's say I want to buy 100 shares of IBM at $124 per
share. I figure out that I will put in a stop order at around
the $121 level. The actual number is something like
$120-7/8. Whole numbers and even fractions are where
the public enters the markets; I stay away from public
orders. There might be a lot of public orders resting at
$121 to buy the stock, but all the orders to buy at that

price won't be filled. If they are all filled at $121, there's a reason why informed insiders would be willing to sell all the public wants to buy at the $121 level. My selling out my position at $120-7/8 would be warranted because the price of the stock should drop pretty drastically after all the public orders to buy at the 121 support level are taken out.

Let's go back to the original scenario, where I buy stock at $124. I now enter an order to stop out my position at $120-7/8. At $120-7/8 I am taking a $3-1/8 risk. If the price does not drop to my stop price, then I must wait patiently for it to go up. The rule that cautions me not to let a profit turn into a loss tells me that once the price of the stock goes above my purchase price I must get rid of it if and when it starts to show a possibility of a loss. *(The rule does not tell me to get out of a winning position if it shows a profit!)* If the price reaches a high of $124-1/8, I must be willing to let it go at $124 if it ever dips back there. At $124-1/4 I must sell it if it gets back to $124. If it shoots up immediately to $130, I must sell it if it gets back to $124!

However, strict adherence to the rule is impractical for two reasons. The first reason is that markets never go straight up or down. If you bought a stock at $124, you can't realistically expect it to go straight up without any backing action. The second reason is that the cost of commissions to the outsider is too high relative to the minimum fluctuations. If commission costs are $50 for a one-sided execution on a 100-share trade at $124, the stock price would have to go up to $125 before you would break even. If you got out of the trade at the same price you went in, you would wind up a loser.

In this example I used a trailing $3-1/8 point stop, or whatever dollar amount I was willing to risk on that type of trade. That is, if the stock trades up to a high price of $125, I would move my stop up to $121-7/8, risking $3-1/8.

If the stock trades up to $126, I would move my stop up to $122-7/8, still risking 3-1/8.

The subjective judgment comes in once the stock trades at or above $125. Here I would risk a potential loss of $2-1/8 from my *original entry* position of $124; at $126 I would risk a potential loss of $1-1/8 from my original entry position of $124. I am making a distinction between potential losses from entry price and the potential loss from the high move. The first case is oriented towards trading equity, independent of market action. In the second case, the profit valuation is based on trading equity plus a portion of the paper profits dependent on the high of the market's up move. My main objective is to preserve my initial equity. If I can maintain control of my equity, I will have greater control over market risks to my paper profits.

In either case—a $125 high or a $126 high—I would risk losing part of my equity. According to Rule 4, any deterioration of trading equity is not acceptable, so with the entry price at $124, my exit point must be at $124 if the trade goes against me. The problem concerns the definition of a loss. At what price level or time span, relative to the entry level of my trade, do I have a loss?

When you put on a trade, the potential loss must be taken out of your trading capital. If you buy stock at $124, you place a stop at a lower price. The difference between the entry price and the stop loss price is your potential loss.

When the trade you have put on starts to show a profit, at what point do you consider the paper profits a part of your trading capital that you can use to gauge potential losses? If the stock you bought at $124 is now at $130 and you still have the open position, you now have a paper profit of $6; on 100 shares of stock you show a profit of $600. At what point do you consider this $600, unrealized as it is, to be part of your trading capital?

This is hard to determine, and since you are dealing with capital, it isn't a question of mere semantics. If you consider your trading capital to be original capital less the paper profit, then you can let the price of the stock dip all the way back to $124 before you start to worry about a deterioration of your trading capital. If, on the other hand, you consider the $600 paper profit to be part of your trading equity, then once the price dips below $130, you will have sustained a loss. I settle on something in the middle when the price appreciates to a level where my position cannot be taken out at a loss if the trailing stop order is executed—I take half of the paper profits, as marked by the extreme of the move and use that as a stop point, give or take a few fractions. That is, with the initial entry price of $124 and a high swing of $130, I would place my stop at around the halfway mark—somewhere slightly below $127: $126-7/8 or $126-3/8. This is a rule of thumb to preserve some sort of profits. The actual stop price might be closer to the lower range of some important chart support point.

I have always chosen the halfway mark as a balance. At a one-half retracement back, you have an even chance of being wrong or right. A one-third retracement back would be giving the market too little leeway in reactions. The market often retraces one-third, only to resume its original direction. If you unload your position at a one-third retracement, you would be selling prematurely out of a bullish move. On the other hand, a two-thirds retracement would be offering the market too much of your profits. I have often found that if the market backs two-thirds, it is too weak to rally much. If this situation occurs, then it is a good idea to close out your positions.

Whatever frame of reference you use to determine whether market retracements have affected your profits, you must do it systematically. You can't consider a dip below the high of the swing to be a loss of profits on one trade and a dip to the halfway mark of your paper profits to be an erosion of profits on the next trade.

A systematic approach to valuing market losses is crucial in evaluating future market trends. The permutations of the markets are infinite and random, whereas the methods of analyzing the markets are finite and must be systematic. Your goal as a successful trader must be to make the market less random and less infinite.

R U L E 5

Trade with the Trend

An experience I had driving the notorious "S" curve on Chicago's Lake Shore Drive about ten years ago showed me that moving with the trend can be a basic survival strategy on many different levels.

Before it was redesigned, this curve was the scene of many accidents because of the two sharp turns that gave it more of a "Z" shape. Returning home after a rough day of trading, I was a bit sloppy in steering the car around the narrow-laned curve. First I crossed the white dividing line on the left; then I overshot the right dividing line in my lane and had to veer again sharply back to the left.

As I shifted the car back and forth, trying to avoid an accident on either side, I had a visual image of what "trading with the trend" was all about. Over the years, this rule helped me make a lot of money in the markets. As long as I stayed within my own lane and progressed with the traffic, I eventually got to the end. When other drivers veered sharply out of their lanes, they crashed into other cars. The markets are similar to this. Once a market is in a defined trend, you must trade with the directions of that market. If you fail to do this, you will have many accidents.

The markets are in one of two stages at any given point in time: They are either trending markets, which are bullish or bearish, or nontrending markets, which trade within a bracketed high and low price range. However, once a market is in an established market type it stays there until it is played out. There are various technical and fundamental indicators that will reveal the approximate time and price at which a trending market will be exhausted and a reversal will take place.

Once a market establishes a trend, it is foolhardy for you, as an off-floor trader, to fade that trend. However, floor traders have always been able to scalp profits from incoming orders by fading the immediate trend. They have some important advantages over off-floor traders.

First of all, the pit trader has more liquidity in trade execution than an off-floor trader could ever have. When a floor trader fades a minor trend by selling contracts at the offered price, he has at his disposal the sell side orders coming into the pit to take him out of a bad trade. He will bid at the bid side, which will probably be under the last sale.

Let's look at an actual example of what a floor trader does: Assume that the market for Treasury bond futures is 90-15/32 bid and offered at 90-16/32. The high for the day is 90-15/32, so the market is moving up at the moment. The trend is short-term bullish. Orders to sell from the outside are coming in and finding buyers in the pit at 90-15/32, the high of the day. It is at this critical juncture of the trading scene that buy and sell orders are perfectly matched, with contracts changing hands at 90-15/32. The floor trader offers bonds at 90-16/32, which if transacted will be a new high price for the day. If the trader had bought at 90-14/32 just before the move to 90-15/32 bid and 90-15/32 offer, when the market action moved to a strong 90-15/32 bid with scattered offers at 90-15/32, he has inventory to sell at 90-16/32. If the strength of the intermediate trend is such that the market moves to 90-15/32 bid and 90-16/32 offered and transacted at the new high price of the day, market orders coming into the pit will be sold at whatever bids are represented in the pit: 90-15/32, and traders will sell out inventory at 90-16/32, giving them an immediate 1/32nd or 2/32nd profit. When the market moves to 90-16/32 bid and 90-17/32 offer, the trader who is short at 90-16/32 will be able to work the orders coming into the pit to sell at whatever the bid is.

Because they can sell at the offered price and buy at the bid price, pit traders can *appear* to trade against the trend and still make profits consistently. Outside traders, on the other hand, can only buy at the offer and sell at the bid price that the pit is currently trading at. They also have to pay a commission to enter the market. This means that there are two strikes against outside traders that will prevent them from trading against any short-term or intermediate trend. In order to overcome these two disadvantages, outside traders must trade with all odds in their favor. This can be done only by buying in a bull market and selling in a bear market. They cannot try to sell and buy like the floor traders who have a short-term frame of reference and an inherent commission advantage.

The strictest definition of a bull market is one in which prices move higher as time passes; in a bear market prices go lower as time passes. The velocity does not detract from the fact that prices will be moving in a trending direction.

Figure 5–1 shows a line sloping upwards at a 45-degree angle. This illustration would be the most middle of the road example of an upward price slope. Prices, however, oscillate around this upward trendline, as shown in Figure 5–2. Figure 5–3 illustrates that the market can be

Figure 5–1.   **A simplistic view of a bull market, shown by an upward-sloping 45° line.**

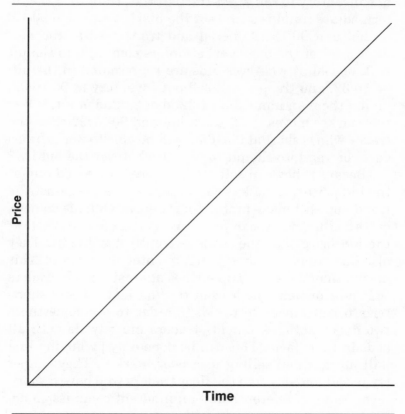

oversold (OS), as shown by the troughs in the oscillating price trends, or overbought, as shown by the peaks in the oscillating price trends (OB).

If you look at the oscillating price movement in the bull trending illustration you can discern that every time price moves up two units, it only retraces one unit and never retraces more than two units. If a bull trend can be defined in such an oscillating fashion, then if you buy every time you have the chance to, your chances for a profit

26

Figure 5–2. **A more detailed chart than Figure 5–1, showing price line oscillating upward around the 45° line in a bull market.**

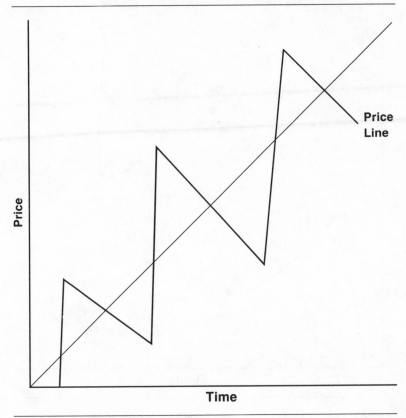

range from a probability of two to one in your favor at best (when oversold), to one to one at worst (when overbought). If you were to sell in a bull market every time you have the chance to, the odds at best would be one to one in your favor of making profits and one to two at worst against you. This type of ratio to profit play is open to every trader, yet most unsuccessful traders do not realize the impact of this little example.

Figure 5–3. A simplistic odds evaluation of the bull market. (OB = overbought; OS = oversold.)

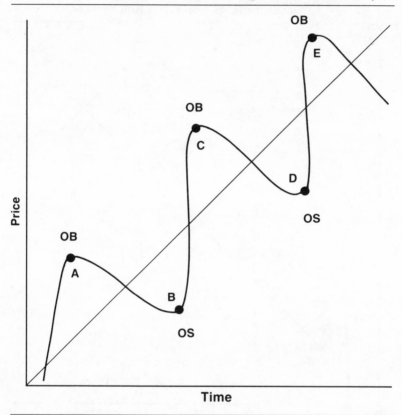

Situation 1: From Price Value A to B to C—Selling Short in a Bull Market.

If you sell in a bull market anywhere from point A to B, you have a maximum profit of one point (if you sell at A) and a minimum profit of zero points (if you sell at B). When price moves from B to C, your loss is two points when price reaches point C. If you sell at the best spot (point A), at C you have a one-point loss. If you sell at B, you have a two-point loss when price moves to C. If you sell at A and cover at B, you have the maximum profit of one point.

Situation 2: From Price Value A to B to C—Buying in a Bull Market.

If you buy instead of sell anywhere between points A and B, the results are dramatically different. If you buy at A and sell out at B, you lose a maximum of one point. If you buy at A and sell out at C, you make one point. If you buy at B, you could make a maximum of two points at price C.

Reverse the situation in bear markets and you will see that if you sold every time you had the opportunity you would automatically have the odds on your side all the time. And if you have the odds in your favor every time you trade, the very fact that there are no supports in bear markets and no resistances in bull markets ensures that you will make money.

RULE 6

If You Don't Know What's Going on, Don't Do Anything

This elementary rule is so familiar to most traders that they give it lip service and dismiss it. But you would be surprised at how often traders get into situations that they have to nurse to profitability by doing exactly what this rule admonishes against.

The problem that most people who try to become successful traders have with this rule is that they will not perform the study that is necessary to make a successful trade until *after* the trade is made. By this time the trader is either nursing a position that is inherently unsound or else he takes profits way too early, both of which are terrible trading strategies.

To illustrate the importance of research, I will compare the mental and physical process of purchasing a household item to that of trading in the markets.

If you were buying a new VCR, for example, you would probably ask your friends for their advice about which brand to purchase and then compare the features of each model they recommend. To fortify your decision you might pick up a copy of some test reports to find out what was written about your choices. You would begin doing this weeks or months before you actually purchased a machine. When you were ready to buy, you would look for a sale at a local department store or check the prices in the advertisements in newspapers and magazines. You would then select the one that has the cheapest prices and the best guarantee protections. Finally, you would use it for about a week to see if it fulfilled your needs in a VCR. If you were unhappy with your purchase you would return it for a refund or a credit against another purchase. That's all there is to purchasing a VCR!

Now let's see what goes on in a stock or futures transaction. Your commodities broker calls you at the office one morning and tells you of a developing situation in the cocoa markets caused by a boll weevil that has been destroying all the crops. Or, if it's your stockbroker, he tells you of the latest rumor on a major acquisition: General Motors, after having failed at bringing in H. Ross Perot to computerize it, is going to make a tender offer for IBM. You know that the profits you could make on either trade would pay for this year's vacation to the Bermudas. Still cautious, you tell your broker you'll think about it and get back to him tomorrow. As the day wears on, the thought of riding a market winner tempts you more. By the time you get home you know you will have to buy a couple of contracts, not just one. Next morning, your broker calls to remind you that the markets are going to open in 15 minutes. Deliberately and methodically he says to you, "Do you want to get on board this winning trade?" You swallow hard. The glowing bodies in the Club Med posters glow back at you. "Yeah, buy me five contracts on the opening." Done.

The first major difference between the VCR purchase and the stock or futures transaction is the time frame. In the case of the VCR, you had ample time to familiarize yourself with the product before making a purchase. In a stock or futures transaction you talk to your broker on the phone and within minutes you are the owner of five cocoa contracts. The broker tries to make it as easy as possible for you to execute trades. Nonetheless, it always seems that when you want fast execution of a trade, your broker's service is not fast enough, but when you need time for strategic consideration of a possible trade, time flies.

The second difference is a psychological one: the greed and fear associated with making money. When you buy a VCR, you actively solicit outside opinions, and people are generally willing to offer you their best advice. When you are buying stocks or futures, on the other hand, you will find that very few people are willing to impart information on how to make money. You yourself might be reluctant to talk about money matters with other people. Some people won't even talk about money with their spouse, yet good advice on trading and speculating is more critical than it is on the purchase of a VCR.

The third difference deals with the nature of the way products and risk vehicles are bought and sold. The VCR is returnable if you aren't happy with it. It's only a loss of your time if you decide to return it within a reasonable period. Stocks and futures contracts are not returnable if you aren't satisfied with your decision. Of course, if the stocks or futures appreciate in price while you are holding them, you stand to gain from that appreciation if you sell your interests to another buyer at the higher price. Why are risk vehicles sold on a no-return basis? Perhaps it is because stocks and futures were designed to be sold rather than bought.

RULE 7

Tips Don't Make You Any Money

Tips are pieces of information that come from questionable sources with no known way of tracing them.

It's not true that tips don't make you any money. Reliable tips can make good money for you. One trader had a tip on American Hospital Supply stock before it was taken over by Baxter Labs several years ago. In less than 24 hours he made $250,000. I've made money on reliable tips, but I've also lost money on tips that turned out bad.

The issue of using tips for profit goes beyond the issue of right or wrong, although tips do present an unfair advantage to investors and traders who are privy to such information. The real issue is the need to function as an independent, self-contained trader. Unlike the role traders take when they actively pursue fundamental or technical research, the traders who seek tips are passive. Once traders relinquish their autonomy by relying on tips, they might as well start to work for someone else. They become, in a sense, employees of the tip giver.

As a long-term trader with a vested interest in the markets, it is better to make money by correctly analyzing the markets yourself. Then you become the master of your own destiny. As you learn to read market action, your skill in the markets is transportable. That is, you can take the knowledge that you have acquired and trade from anywhere in the world without having to rely on tips. Conceptually and practically, all markets behave in the same manner. Once you know how to trade successfully, you can transfer correct trading practices from one market to another with ease.

On the other hand, if you learn to make money by relying on tips, you are no longer free to trade any market. You are dependent on your source, who in turn is dependent on his or her source, and so on, upwards to the ultimate source. The chain of tip givers must not be broken if you are to continue to make profits on tips. As an independent trader I find this situation confining.

In the realm of market analysis, the trader takes in all the information that he or she has access to in order to arrive at a decision to buy or sell particular markets. The type of information the trader inputs into his or her analysis falls into two types: technical data and fundamental data. These data are available to everyone, and the sources of the data are continuous and credible. Knowing how to read the data is a specialized skill that you learn and can implement in the market every day. Not so with reliance on tips.

The argument for using tips is that you can take one tip and ride it all the way to several hundred thousand dollars or millions of dollars of profits. However, in the process of making all these ill-gotten gains, you forget about doing anything else. You no longer try to apply fundamental or technical analysis to market situations. You no longer treat the market as a business.

Those who do get burned by tips are too embarrassed to talk about it and also are afraid to cut off the source of their tips, bad as they might be. Bad information from fundamental sources will eventually stop because of market forces. Traders will stop paying for such information. The same applies to bad technical analysis techniques. If a trading technique is flawed, market forces will shunt it aside in favor of better ones. The dynamics of tip giving and receiving are not subject to the natural selection process of the marketplace. Good tips are given to only a few. Bad tips are given to everyone.

The next time you hear a tip, check the source. It might be a distribution of stocks or futures by the tipsters.

R U L E 8

Use the Right Orders To Get into the Markets

There are many types of orders that you can give your broker to execute, depending on what you want to do and how you want to do it. You must use the right type of order to get the right results.

Most of my orders are market orders. If I want to get into a position, I enter a market order at the prevailing price. Conversely, if I want to liquidate my position, I do it at the market. My feeling has always been to get a position in the market: If bullish, I want to own something, and if bearish, I want to sell something.

Most traders do not like to execute their orders at the market price but at a limit price. These traders are really saying that the likely market scenario, either continuation of a bullish or bearish move, won't occur until their price limit is reached. This type of thinking implies that the market will act according to the trader's wishes. This is patently absurd. The market will do what it wants to do. It is the role of the trader to figure out what the markets are doing in order to profit from them.

There are times when orders other than market orders are not only preferred, but required for good trade execution. Following are the most common types of orders and the market conditions under which they may be used.

Limit Orders. These orders specify execution at a certain price limit. A buy limit order would direct the executing broker to buy at a specified price limit. A sell limit order specifies the price at which an issue should be sold. If the price of the issue is currently at $24 and you tell a broker that you want to buy a certain amount at $22, your broker will not try to execute the order unless it first reaches $22, and you won't be guaranteed an execution until it goes below $22. The converse is true in bull markets where you enter orders to sell at a fixed price greater than the current market price.

Limit orders are like trading blindfolded. If the price of a stock is at $24, but you feel that $22 is a fairer price, then this is not the right time to buy it. If you give a limit order to your broker to buy it at $22, you're saying that you won't be around to watch the stock go to $22 but want your broker to represent you when it reaches that price. If it goes to $22 when you're not watching it, what makes you think that the conditions that were present when the stock was at $24 did not change to new conditions that might make the stock a less attractive purchase at the lower price of $22? In short, when you tell your broker to buy or sell something at a price that is not at the current market, you're telling him to execute your trade and ignore whatever new reasons there might be to explain why the price has changed.

Market-if-Touched (MIT). An MIT order is executed at the prevailing market price when a price limit that you determined ahead of time is reached. This is to differentiate it from the limit order, which is executed at a fixed price once that price is reached. Market-if-touched orders are used in markets that swing from liquidity to illiquidity. The price action will encounter pockets of extreme to moderate activity, depending on where prices are at the time. Implied in an MIT order is that once your limit is reached, you want your order to be filled at any price. You don't want to hang around with your order until another price level is reached.

I have often used MIT orders in the bond futures market closes. The last 15 minutes of trading are often hectic if the futures start to trade strongly in one direction. Before the last quarter hour I look at the high or low of the day and enter an MIT order just slightly above either side of the range. If I am long and want to liquidate the long, I enter an MIT order several ticks above the high of the day if the market appears to be ready to charge into new high territory. If the market has enough strength to punch through new highs at the last quarter hour of trading, it often represents some sort of hectic rush to buy, perhaps a panic short covering rally. I want my order to be offered at the market once the limit is reached so that I can squeeze a few extra ticks out of it. It's not surprising to see the price jump by two to three ticks under such closing price conditions. The alternative is to wait until a few minutes before the close time and rush in a market order; this approach puts too much pressure on the phone clerks and the executing broker on the floor. I like to ease the task of the order takers so that they don't make mistakes that I often have to pay for.

Contingency Orders. These are composites of two different types of orders based on sympathetic markets that follow the movements of other markets: Silver follows gold, the Dow Jones industrials follows the Dow Jones transportations, wheat futures follow oat futures, etc. When a limit price or a certain market condition is

41

reached on the first order, the second order is executed. Most exchanges do not allow such orders, but you can create a hybrid order if you can get your broker to handle it.

To illustrate how a contingency order is created let's take a look at orders to buy silver futures based on the strength of gold prices. Your broker tracks the price of gold. Once a gold price limit is reached, he goes to the second part of your order and attempts to execute the order to buy silver. Your order might read: "Buy five February delivery month of silver futures at the market contingent on May delivery month of gold futures reaching $420." If the gold futures trade at $420 or above after your order is entered, then it is incumbent on the retail broker to send an order into the silver pit to buy your five contracts. If a floor broker is willing to accept the order, the floor broker in the silver pit will be executing the order and monitoring the gold prices. Most floor brokers are too busy to handle such orders, but retail brokers can generally take this order because they have the price monitoring equipment available. Of course, don't expect your retail broker to monitor the prices of both markets in order to execute such an order.

I seldom use contingency orders because they are very messy to follow and track. If there is a mistake on the execution, it is difficult to obtain times and sale prices to support any arguments. Why bother when it's so much easier to enter your positions at the market?

One Cancels the Other. This is a real strange order. Again, there are two types of orders involved here. It's also a contingency order where if either the first or the second order's conditions are met, then the remaining order, the second or the first, is cancelled.

I have used these orders to buy or sell a futures contract when I had no preference on the delivery month. If the first two delivery months are trading freely, I enter an order to buy either the first one if its price is reached or the second one if its price is reached. Once one order is executed, the other is cancelled. I have never had both orders filled at the same time because there is only one executing broker for this type of order. If two brokers in two different markets were executing the order, then it is possible that both orders could be filled, but no broker would take such an order because he or she would be forced to rely on another broker for an execution.

Fill or Kill (FOK). I used to use this type of order until I realized that it doesn't give any better fills and only aggravates the traders and market makers. The order is entered into the trading pit or to the specialist like any other order, except that all the conditions of the order have to be met or else it is cancelled, or killed. There is no such thing as a partial fill or a fill at varying prices. An FOK order could read: "Buy 30 January soybeans at $5.60, fill or kill." The executing floor broker offers to buy all 30 contracts at $5.60, and will not accept 10 contracts at $5.55, 10 at $5.60, and 10 at $5.65 for an average price of 30 at $5.60. Fill or kill orders have been used because some traders who want an execution right then and there will enter the fill or kill component to the order because of slow reporting procedures. I also did that until my broker caught on to what I was doing.

When you decide to enter the market, your role is to put on a position in the market, not to mastermind how you will obtain your order. A market order is the best way to obtain a position in the market. There are rare occasions under which you can use other orders, more in the areas of exiting your trades than in entering your trades. If you have to be fancy about entering orders, use a market order to enter your position and use the other orders to exit.

RULE 9

Don't Be Whimsical about Closing out Your Trades

Traders spend a good portion of their waking hours analyzing the markets. They try to determine how they can enter the markets correctly, yet they spend very little time planning what to do if their analysis is wrong. They also don't predetermine points where they can take profits.

Initiating a trade is only one part of the total process. There are really three parts to a trade: 1) decision making, 2) execution, and 3) management. Each part is critical to successful trading, and each part must follow in sequence. However the only part that makes money is the management part.

The first part of the trade is decision making. Most traders learn techniques of fundamental and technical analysis to help them decide whether they should go long or short in a trade. It takes a long time to gain knowledge in this area, and the learning curve is steep. Hence, this part of the trade makes no money for the trader.

In fundamental analysis the trader analyzes the balance sheets and income statements of companies to predict future price movements of the stocks. The analyst tries to predict future trends in past assets, earnings, sales, products, management, markets, and other indicators. He or she assesses whether a particular stock or group of stocks is undervalued or overvalued at the current market price. The fundamentalist analyzes commodities, interest rates, and foreign currencies with these tools.

The technical analyst, on the other hand, looks at supply and demand in terms of price, time, and volume action. The analyst tries to discover repeatable patterns by charting these types of data. Once the analyst classifies price, time, or volume action into repeatable patterns, he or she can then forecast future patterns.

Traders cannot learn fundamental or technical analysis overnight. From my own experience, it takes several years to become proficient with these tools. The time spent learning the analytical tools causes many traders to overemphasize this portion of a trade.

The second part of a trade is the execution. Although this part of the trade can be learned within a month, it also does not make the trader any money; at best, it will reduce price skids on trades. After the trader has decided to either buy or sell, there is a spectrum of approaches to executing the trade. The trader can enter a trade at the market price or at a limit price; he can enter a long position with a stop buy order or a short position with a stop sell order; he can close out a position at the market with a stop on the close only; he can place contingency orders; he can buy at noon and sell 15 minutes before the close, etc.

Sometimes traders confuse the decision-making tools with the trade execution tools and begin to view the execution part of the trade to be the same as the decision-making part. These traders end up trading more often than they should and for much less profit than they can get.

The third part of the trade is the management of the position. This part makes all the money. It is the most critical part of a *successful* trade. Successful traders handle this part well. Unsuccessful traders are unaware that this portion of a trade exists.

When the trade turns into a profit, the unsuccessful trader takes his profits; the winning trader tries to determine whether or not the trade will continue to show more profits. If it shows promise of more profits, the trader allows it to run its course.

Losing trades don't start as large losses, but as controllable small losses. When unsuccessful traders have a small loss, they allow it to expand. If they want to move into the winners' class, they must learn to manage their trades correctly.

Of the three parts of a trade, position management requires the least amount of study, for there is nothing to study, yet it is the only part that can make the profit. The part that does require study is the study of yourself and your own personality traits. You must know how comfortable you are with yourself as a winner, how you cope with failure, and how you handle disagreements in life.

It is difficult not to lump the three parts of a trade together because the decision-making process takes the longest time to learn. However, a trader who becomes consumed by the act of deciding doesn't know what to do with the trade once it is executed. If the decision to enter the trade is incorrect, the trader does not know how to get out and allows the losses to compound. If the decision to enter the trade is correct, the trader does not know how to manage the position. He or she sells out too soon and prevents the profits from accruing.

When you learn the process of making a trade over several years, the three parts to a trade appear to overlap to the point where you cannot see their demarcations. The next time you want to make a trade, decide what you want to do based on fundamental analysis, technical analysis, or a combination; then execute the trade. Finally, bring out your desire to make a profit: Manage the position correctly. Remember that when you start a trade, you are only partially on the way on the road to wealth!

RULE 10

Withdraw a Portion of Your Profits

The business of trading is very profitable when you know what to do in the markets. Unlike other businesses, when you don't know what you are doing in the trading business, your losses are unlimited and can come along rapidly. In other businesses when you don't know what you are doing you can buy talent to mitigate the losses. In trading, you have only yourself to rely upon.

Because they have learned to rely on themselves, traders have rather large egos, especially after successfully completing a trading campaign. We need to reward ourselves for doing well in the markets, but the rewards must be translated into tangible things. Money in a trading account is not a tangible item. Buy yourself nice clothes, take a well-deserved vacation, or buy a new car.

What you mustn't do is to reward yourself by taking bigger market risks. When you do make money trading, you must take a portion of the profits out and put it in a separate account. This is an absolute requirement for your long-term stability in the business. The role of a professional speculator is to reduce trading risks in market positions, even to the point of limiting the capital that they have in their trading accounts.

I can hear a reader saying, "When I have the money in my account, I can take on bigger positions so that I can make the million dollar trades." This is a valid thought. However, please note that I suggest that you take out a *portion* of your profits, not all of your profits. In this manner, you will still have a portion of your profits to trade increasingly larger positions following successful trades. With this cautiously risk-reducing attitude towards profits, you'll have money to spend if you're unlucky enough to run through a series of bad trades.

The bottom line to making more money in the markets is to increase trading size, but this must be coupled with good market analysis. Some unsuccessful traders mistakenly believe that they can avoid increasing trading size by merely increasing frequency. (When I see floor traders suddenly jump from low activity to high activity, they are probably in trouble with their positions.) Every time a trader has a position in the marketplace, there is always risk. The only way to have no risk is to have no positions. As an aside to what is the correct way to increase your trading position I have several thoughts.

When you initiate longs at the beginning of a bull move you trade the number of positions that your account can handle; however, you're always wondering when the position will turn into a profit so that you can parlay that profit into more positions. For whatever the reasons, we find ourselves sticking profits into our trading account so that we can accumulate more positions on the long side. At the beginning and bottom of the move we are long one contract. At the top of the move, with its inevitable reversal, we are long 50 contracts. As the market gets closer to the top, we should be long only one contract. And at the beginning and bottom of the move we should be long 50 contracts.

One of the best investments that one can make with the profits is to take long, relaxing vacations. The irony of this business is that most unsuccessful traders will take vacations when they can least afford them: when they have just been nailed in the markets. After losing a bundle in the markets, some traders will dig into their trading account for a few thousand dollars to pay for a trip to Club Med or the Bahamas. After losing such an amount, they are more than willing to be away from trading, although this further depletes their trading capital. Had the partial profits been taken out when there were some, the losing traders could have tapped this reserve fund without having to go into their trading account for more money. As you will see in other chapters, the psychology of separating types of funds to trade with, types of funds to invest with, and types of funds to pay living expenses with, etc., affect you as a trader. Capital that is stashed away somewhere where it cannot be touched by an adverse market move gives the trader confidence to weather bad market situations.

Some traders reward themselves on both the tangible level and the risk level: They take the long vacation or buy the expensive sports car, and they also take the bigger trading risks. This is a very bad way to approach the investment of one's profits. The cost for the long vacation or the car is a one-time expense, but the risk of trading capital can be recurring. How many times have we heard of traders who can't afford to trade any more because they took a hit in the markets? Had they stashed away their investments and capital, they would have had reserves to fall back on.

If you make $2,000 profits in a $10,000 trading account, you have made a 20 percent return on your total risk capital. If you continue to trade and view your total risk capital as $12,000, you have increased the amount of your risk capital to 120 percent of your original $10,000. On the other hand, if you had withdrawn half of your trading profits, $1,000, you would have $11,000 to continue to trade with, and $1,000 stashed away or invested. You will be surprised at how good it feels to have that $1,000 stashed away.

A good rule of thumb is to withdraw half of your profits out of your trading account every month and completely ignore the amount withdrawn. Consider only how much is in your trading account as the risk capital. If you follow this rule, you will be able to consistently make money from the markets instead of consistently contributing to the health and wealth of other traders.

One trader I know always takes out a portion of his profits every month. One month he pulled out enough profits to buy a cabin in Wisconsin. Another month he pulled out profits to buy a racing boat. He doesn't follow the percentage rule strictly, but he pulls out a portion of his profits on a consistent basis. The last six months, the markets have been dull and he hasn't had the profits to pull out. But he does have the cabin in Wisconsin and his racing boat to help him patiently wait out the next market moves. He isn't forced to push the markets for moves that aren't there. If he hadn't invested part of his profits in this manner, he would have taken a few shots here and there, increasing his chances of losing money by trying to force the markets to make money for him when it isn't possible.

RULE 11

Don't Buy a Stock Only To Obtain a Dividend

This chapter should be titled "Be Careful of Inducements Offered to Purchase a Stock, Especially Dividends." There are so many ways the marketers of stocks make their product more attractive to prospective purchasers that a whole book on marketing the stock market would be the only way to do the subject justice.

The public investor perceives that one of the reasons for stock ownership is the return on an investment. This can be as simple as the quarterly dividend paid out to holders of the stock or as complicated as factoring in the profits accrued from a covered write into the capital gains of the underlying stock. In the former case, the dividend is issued from the company itself. In the latter, additional profits are accumulated through the investor's own acumen.

I personally would rather rely on the investor's own acumen. I've never heard of any company management who consistently did anything for the strict benefit of the stockholders. For all practical purposes, ownership of the working operations of companies is never transferred to stockholders because their ownership is fragmented. Stockholder control can be implemented through the accumulation of enough voting rights, but getting enough stockholders together to make their voting rights count is tantamount to a complete reorganization of the company. Management still owns the right to control the destiny of the company.

The stock market is more complex than the futures markets or other capital markets because of the inducements that make them appealing to various groups of prospective purchasers. In the futures markets, the appeal to prospective purchasers are broken down into two aspects of an equation: supply and demand.

In the stock markets, there are many different groups of potential buyers: people who buy stocks because they want to have capital gains; people who buy stocks because some interesting news captured their interest; people who buy stocks to take advantage of arbitrage plays; and people who buy stocks to obtain dividends. Each group can be lured into the marketing of stocks at different entry points in the cycle. These people with diverse interests can be further broken down into two categories: capital gains players and return on investment players.

Let's analyze the creation of stock for the purpose of making it available on the open market. Once you see how the markets are structured you will see how dividends enter into the game of marketing stocks. There are several important facts to realize about the marketing of stocks: Who is selling the stock, and who is buying it? If you owned a privately held company and you were selling some or all of your company to someone else, would you sell your company at bargain prices or would you try to get the best possible price for it?

Marketing has to be implemented by the owners. They have interests in the company, and they would like to convert that ownership to cash. The cleverest owners also are able to retain absolute control of the companies they once owned but now manage "on behalf of the stockholders": They use the assets of the company and the assets of the new shareholders to enrich themselves.

Like retail advertising, stock marketing has a language of its own. Instead of saying "comparable to a higher priced item," which a department store would say to sell its refrigerators, the stock marketer says "now selling at a fraction of its all-time high." Take a look at the following list of comparable marketing messages.

Department Store	Stock Marketer
New and improved	New oil discoveries
Guaranteed to enhance your life	Looks like another Xerox
Inventory cleanup	Quarterly housecleaning
Buy one, get one free	Stock split
Heavy duty	Blue-chip defensive issue
High-quality at a value price	AAA rating with high return
Incredibly new	New issues with potentials
Sensational savings	An insider buying chance
Extra-strength	Overbought
Last call for savings	Challenging former highs
More for less	Hard asset play
Extra nutrition	Undervalued assets
Nothing protects better	Virtually no downside
Ouchless	No margin calls
100% natural	No market makers in this
No preservatives	No strings attached
Clinically tested mild	Research analysts recommend
Easy to use—no mess	Just sign the account forms
We sell excitement	Glamour stock situation
Less fat	Turnaround situation
Compare and save	Buy the leading issue

An investor who realizes that stocks are products to be marketed develops a healthy skepticism about the "advertising" that goes on in marketing the stocks. The wise investor knows how to read between the lines.

It should come as no surprise to readers that stocks are sold initially at very dear prices, just as department store products are marked up for sale to the customers. The founding owners of a company sell stocks of ownership at very high prices. Shortly after this point, bargains for the company's stock are available. There are exceptions, such as the new issues of Apple Computer, but for the most part stocks can be bought cheaper after the initial offering.

Bargains for stocks exist in one of two ways or a combination of the two: current owners, be they the founders or mere shareholders, unload stocks at below liquidation prices, or the company improves and grows while the stock price fails to respond to the fundamental changes.

It is a bad investment to buy stocks at above valuation prices, or at overvaluation, at any stage of the marketing cycle. This gives you less potential for profits because the upside price moves would be limited. There are many ways that the stock marketer will make it easy for you to believe that the current overvaluation of the price is justified, when it isn't the case.

Increasing a dividend on a stock is a mechanical way of making a stock more appealing for prospective investors. These prospects, however, are also sensitive to obtaining a rate of return for their investments. If a company increases a dividend, it can just as easily decrease it. However, investors who are looking for returns on capital can mistakenly assume that once a dividend is declared the dividend payments will continue. Woe to the investor who buys a stock because of a dividend increase and finds that the dividend is later cancelled!

RULE 12

Don't Average Your Losses

How many times have you had a position go against you? You planned the trade correctly, but soon after you bought your initial position, you discovered that the price you paid was higher than what it was now worth. The first trade was a loser compared to market price.

What could you do with this losing trade? You could sell it out and look to buy something else, or you could buy a few more shares or contracts at the now lower price. Which is the better solution to your dilemma? In most cases, I would suggest that you either cut your losses by selling out your position or else stay with the losing position.

Most people, however, would buy more at lower prices. They would average their losses on the way down if they are buying, or average their losses on the way up if they are shorting. There's an old saying that if it looked good at a higher price, it looks a lot better at a bargain price. This approach can work at times, but usually it won't.

Traders determine whether they will average or not by looking at what they are trading: stocks, options, or futures. Let's look at each of these trading vehicles in terms of averaging losses.

When dealing with stocks, averaging losses at lower prices can often work, depending on the viability of the company you are averaging your position in. This means that the company you are buying mustn't go bankrupt or in any way destroy your ownership interest. If there is even a slight chance that your stock will become worthless through bankruptcy, you will never get back your investment.

If another company buys or merges with your company, the acquiring company either converts your ownership to a portion of the new company or pays you cash. You will have to average your losses in the newly formed company or else you will be cashed out and will realize a loss on your holdings in the original company. Investors who average their losses will do whatever they can to avoid this. After incurring forced losses due to mergers or buyouts, these investors will forsake their original plan to average their losses and will take the tendered cash to buy stock in the new company or to invest in other companies.

If you are averaging your losses in options, you must realize that this trading instrument has a decaying market value. It is best not to average on the buy side because if you are buying options, you will be adding to a position that will expire worthless. The intrinsic value of the option is based on how much the option is in-the-money. How much remains after the decay in the time value of the option? You won't have a chance to hang on to your position.

On the short side, you can sell options naked. If the position goes against you, you can sell more options, expecting that expiration will reduce your liability. However, not all options situations can be handled this way; you must evaluate each one separately. Suffice it to say that selling options that are going against you requires both intestinal fortitude and deep trading pockets to sustain the losses.

When I traded equity options at the Chicago Board Options Exchange, I knew a trader named Mort Miller, whose predominant strategy was selling strangles and straddles. For some years, underlying stocks gradually moved either up or down—the key word here is *gradually*. The decay in option premium over time made Mort a lot of money.

Mort called me aside one day in early 1987 and asked me to help him out. He told me he was just recuperating from a heart attack and couldn't seem to do anything right in the markets. The markets of 1986–1987 had moved straight up, which meant that one side of Mort's strangles always decayed in value while the other side always amounted to huge losses. For a while Mort continued to sell more options to average his losses on the side that appreciated in value. But as the market started to slow down, the short positions he had averaged his losses on would eventually decay to zero worth.

If he had only looked at the condition and stage of the stock markets, he would have realized that selling straddles and strangles was no longer profitable. In our discussion, Mort and I agreed on one thing: If you have enough money in your account, you can always average your positions in options by selling more options. The key words here are *if you have enough money in your account*. All you have to do is wait until expiration to force your total short position to zero value. That early portion of 1987 was enough for Mort to put all his capital to test in the markets.

When averaging your losses in commodities, remember that commodities will always have some market value. Soybeans and grains will always have some value. Unlike stocks, if you average commodities, you do not have to worry that the price of your investment will go down to zero. What you do have to consider is the expiration of your contracts. The markets will force you to take physical delivery of your commodities, so you must have a lot of money. Average good faith deposits amount to about 10 percent of the market value of the contract. This barely covers your positions if you have sustained losses in your account while averaging your losses. The margin clerk will ask you to come up with the other 90 percent of your original contracts' total value.

When they trade in commodities, most investors and speculators rarely consider that they are playing these markets at a fraction of the total value of the contracts. Unfortunately, when it's time to take delivery of these commodities, most undercapitalized players, up against the trading giants, will not be able to ante up.

In each of the three cases, stocks, options, or futures, the initial consideration in averaging losses was whether or not the total investment or speculation could possibly disappear to zero value. With stocks, this was possible only if the company went bankrupt. With options, you could possibly average your losses only if you were a naked seller. Even with the zero-value consideration in mind, it would be rather risky. Though commodities always have intrinsic worth, it is extremely unlikely that the traders who speculate and try to average their losses would have enough capital to take physical delivery of the commodities at expiration.

Few players have the capital strength to take physical delivery of commodities. Those who do can make some interesting plays. I learned of one profitable risk-free interest rate play from a founder of a national television broadcasting firm. He was a speculator in silver and gold futures contracts at the New York Commodity Exchange and the London Metals Exchange.

The play was basically an arbitrage. When prices got too high in either New York or London, relative to the other exchange, he would sell those contracts and buy the undervalued contract. He would factor the cost of carrying the metals based on interest rates at the time. He would take physical delivery if the profits were there. With metals, physical delivery was the exception rather than the rule. Producers of the metals would have their holdings on deposit in the vaults of one of the exchanges. When traders made delivery, a certificate changed hands from seller to buyer; hence, there was no real physical movement of the metals. This arbitrage play was only available to speculators of his size, with the capital to take delivery of the metals and hold on to them while waiting for the hedged side of the transaction to be delivered at expiration. He was consistently able to make a 4 percent or better rate of return over the risk-free, 90-day T-bill rate. Unfortunately most such plays are not possible for the average speculator.

You often don't know that you have averaged your losses until it's too late because of the many subtleties involving the number and timing of your contracts. First, you must establish your contract size. How many contracts do you trade when you begin? If you commit to buy one contract, there is no need to average. You don't have to buy more either in the direction of the market in your favor or against the market. If you trade more than one contract at a time, then you can and should average your position. If you are a 50-lot trader, you can buy all 50 at a single price or you can ease yourself in at several different prices.

Let's say that you want to buy a position on a particular day because some of your indicators point to a valid buy area. If you buy part of your position at one price, you then have the option of spreading out the balance over many prices. If you average the balance of your total trading position at lower prices, does this mean that you are

61

averaging your losses? Technically speaking, I would say yes. However, from the perspective of your whole trading strategy, you have established an average price for your total commitment in relation to the current market. If you were to add another sized contract the next day at a lower price away from the average of your first commitment or at a different time interval that same day, then I would say that you were averaging your losses. Be sure to make this subtle, but very critical, distinction.

Another point to keep in mind is the major difference between averaging your losses and pyramiding your position. In averaging your losses, you are acquiring more positions when prices are going against the intermediate trend. In pyramiding, you are adding to your position in the direction of the intermediate trend. I will discuss pyramiding extensively in Rule 17.

Another form of averaging losses entails selling another option month or contract to spread off risk. This is done every day in exchange trading pits. It simply requires the trader to concentrate buying in one option, commodity month, or stock and selling in another option, commodity month, or stock.

As an example, a trader concentrates on buying the January soybeans contracts, averaging his losses. He maintains knowledge of the bid and ask of the next commodity month, the May soybeans contracts. (Here, we also talk about the carrying charge markets versus non-carrying charge markets.) As the trader maintains and adds to his inventory of January soybeans contracts at whatever prices, he offers May soybeans at the offered price. If an order that bids up the May soybeans comes into the exchange pit, the trader will find himself locked into a spread position. He is long the January soybeans and short the May soybeans. The soybean market is a carrying charge market, hence defined factors, rather than random market movements, go into the cost of carrying the soybeans from January to May. The difference in price between January and May soybeans is stable. The trader reverses the process when he takes profits. He bids for the May soybeans by averaging down and offers the January soybeans at the offering price. Spreading off averaged positions is viable only if the commission costs are negligible, and even then, the trader is working on razor thin profits in very liquid markets. I don't suggest that the upstairs trader do this type of trading.

Although this strategy of spreading off averaged positions works best in carrying charge markets, it is also used in non-carrying charge markets such as the meats traded at the Chicago Mercantile Exchange. The trader must be fully aware that the difference in price from one delivery month to another is never stable. This instability of price relationships merely adds to the riskiness of this strategy. Instead of dealing in only one contract month, the spread trader in such markets brings in the tentativeness of an unstable spread risk.

If you have been following my train of thought up to this point, you are probably wondering how you can make big money in the markets with only a small winning position. It's fine to be right on a five lot in the Treasury bond futures, but it's better to be able to add to your position and be long 50 contracts for a price move in your favor. Well, the correct way to add to your position is not by averaging your losses. By doing so, you are buying in the opposite direction of a market's intermediate move. Start on a very conservative basis for your first commitment. Ride the position to the top and then take profits. On the next move up, increase your initial commitment. For example, in the first go-around you buy 10 bonds and watch it go up. You take profits and either short or get out of the market completely. When the bonds bottom out, you then buy 20 bonds as an initial commitment. You ride this bond commitment to the top and then sell out. When you are able to do this again and again, you will increase your size to the point that a move can mean hundreds of thousands of dollars to you. This strategy will limit your losses to only a fraction of your total trading commitment.

RULE 13

Take Big Profits and Small Losses

We have read this rule many times, yet many people don't really understand it. If we did, most of us would have profits in our trading accounts instead of losses.

If you are an off-floor trader, the first obstacle to following this rule is your broker. A broker's profits are not based on what you make, but on the number of transactions you have going in your account. If your broker executes your trade and it is an immediate loser, he or she will tell you to wait out the trade so that you can get back to even. This is a bad approach because I have found that the first loss is usually the smallest. Unknowingly, your broker can cause your losing position, which started out as a small loss, to become a larger loss. The broker says that the loss will be made up over time, but how do you know that the markets will accommodate you?

If the trade shows a profit, your broker will be the first to tell you that "You will never go broke taking a profit." This is true, but this is not the way to make big money.

Profits, when you are able to cash out of them, mean that your account has increased in size, but this is only part of the profit-making equation. If all your losses are as big, dollarwise, as your wins, there is some justification for ringing the cash register every time you can; but most traders and investors find that their losses are bigger than their profits on a per trade basis. Because of this imbalance, I try to squeeze whatever I can out of a profitable trade.

When taking profits I use a strategy that is based on simple logic. If the position shows a profit immediately, I unload part of the position. That is, if I am showing profits on 400 shares of stocks or 40 futures contracts, I can ring the register by selling half the position. Depending on how badly I want to get rid of my profitable positions and how comfortable I feel with the actual position, I vary the percentage I sell, but I never sell the full position. I have discovered that when I do have a profitable position on and I am trading correctly with the market trend, I make substantially more money on the balance of my position than I did on the part that I sold.

If you have to do something to an existing position that is showing a profit, you can add on to it. Selling out a profitable position is a tendency in human nature that will prevent you from ever making any substantial profits. It is better to buy more instead of selling out your position totally. If you can't do this, then sell out only part of the position.

The caveat here is that your analysis of the market trend, the consideration of your trading equity at risk, and your current trading experiences must all lean in the direction of your market position. If you are long, make sure you are in a bull market, or at least that it is towards the tail end of a correction in a bull market. You can determine the current stage of market action by using various technical analysis tools. If you want to add to a profitable position, you must make sure you have enough equity in your trading account to cover the additional positions. This is extremely important because you must be able to add more positions without endangering the holding power of your total position. Rule 17 on pyramiding will help you understand what is involved in adding to your position.

Finally, your frame of mind must be good. If you have just experienced a string of losses and now find yourself in a profitable initial position, do you add on more positions? If you are disciplined enough to regard the previous losses as independent market actions that have no direct bearing on your current position, then you can go ahead. Most people, however, will carry their previous experience of losses into the current situation and will either overstay their position or overtrade their equity.

Second comes the psychology of profits and losses. Like everything else in life, your profit taking must be based on long-term plans. When you have a loser, your broker might tell you to hang in there, and you might think that your loser, given time, will come back. Or perhaps you think that you will offset your long-term losses against profits for a favorable tax treatment. It is exactly this treatment of losses that you must guard against. Losses must not be treated like profits. Instead, you must look at losses from a short-term perspective. If you lose money on a trade, you must get out of that trade immediately. Don't rationalize that these losses, given time, will be able to work themselves out over time. Profits, on the other hand, must be treated with a long-term view. If a trade works out to your favor, you must allow it to stay on the books and continue making money for you. Remember: losses must be treated with a short-term perspective and profits must be viewed as long-term situations.

David Garland, a fellow Treasury bond trader at the Chicago Board of Trade, made money by scalping the markets every day for a number of years. One day he was incensed about his day's trading. He sold the top of the bond move. He had unloaded 30 bonds right on the high of the move.

He said he sold the 50 lot at 89-12/32 and covered the 30 bonds at 89-10/32. He made two ticks on 30 contracts, which wasn't a bad day's trade. It was 60 ticks at $31.25, or something like $1,800. The bomb was that the bonds were now at 85-10/32, or four points lower. Each point represented $1,000, so on the 30 contracts he could have made $120,000 in three days. He sold the high tick but only made two ticks profit per contract. Three days later, it could have turned into a profit of $4,000 per contract.

I told him that he had no right to complain about his lost profit potential. After all, as a scalper he makes trades every day, looking to make only a few ticks here and there. If he does enough volume he will make a very good living by scalping ticks. When he sold the top tick, he was a scalper. When he covered his shorts two ticks lower, he was still a scalper. But when he complained about the four points he could have made on the 30 lots, he was thinking like a position trader. As a position trader, he would have been able to carry the position to three days and make the full four points on each contract, but he would have had to come up with the margin money to handle the three days' maintenance. As a position trader, he would not have had the chance to short on the high tick. Position traders do not think like this. Scalpers do.

As a scalper David scalped into the high tick, but he wanted to ride the position as a position trader. This requires tremendous discipline. I have yet to find a trader who can do both well. You are either a scalper or a position trader. You are either a position trader or a day trader. You cannot be both in the same role.

As an outside trader, you can do this by opening two separate accounts and treating one as a trading account and the other as an investment account. You can trade IBM in one account and position IBM in another account, each with its own approach. If IBM seems like a bad day trade, close it out of the trading account, but if it looks like a good long-term hold, stick it in the long-term account and forget about the minor fluctuations that a day trader would worry about.

Once you condition yourself to think along these lines with the separate accounts, you will find it easier to cut your losses when you are wrong and let your profits run when you are right.

RULE 14

Go for the Long Pull as an Outside Speculator

I started trading for my own account in the early 70s, when I bought a membership at the Chicago Open Board of Trade for $4,600. The Open Board was an exchange that traded the job lot contracts of the Chicago Board of Trade futures. Its claim to fame was that traders who started there and did well eventually went over to the Chicago Board of Trade. It was a testing ground for young talent.

Shortly after I became a member, the exchange changed its name to the MidAmerica Commodity Exchange. Several years ago the MidAmerica Commodity Exchange became associated with the Chicago Board of Trade. Now MidAm members trade in a separate room of the Chicago Board of Trade.

I learned a lot from the little exchange. I learned the value of patience. Patience, a very subtle investment approach, is something that we all know about but seldom practice.

The Open Board hired clerical help called "board markers," to record prices. They ranged in age from the very young to the very old. They checked for prices that flashed across the tape at the main exchanges and recorded them by hand on the blackboard.

I became friends with one of the board markers. His surname was Anderson, and everyone called him Andy. Andy was about 5'4". He seldom shaved, and he wore a battered trading jacket that peeled off his thin body. With his bad right leg he hobbled around the pits. He always hunched over as if he were looking for loose change on the floor. When I first met him he was in his late sixties.

He literally got paid nickels and dimes. At lunch time he would order lunch for the traders for a 50-cent fee. He had a pocketful of drinking straws and would sell one to you for three cents. After the markets closed, he would go over to the exchanges and pick up the free bulletins and trading data sheets. Then he would bring them over to the MidAm and sell them for a nickel apiece.

We became good friends, and I learned that Andy was a surprisingly wealthy man. Over the years he continued to add to his net worth. He never made any money in the commodities markets. He made his fortune in stocks. He took care of his older brother. His brother passed away several years ago and Andy, because of his lonely life, passed away by himself. He was a strange but lovable character.

In his youth he had been a clerk to old man Armour, the meatpacker. Andy saw how Armour caused his own demise. Armour figured that after World War II there would be more demand for red meats, so he went long the meats right after the war. His analysis was incorrect. Prices went down. Instead of liquidating his positions at a small loss, Armour bought more. At night Andy would go to Armour's safe-deposit vaults with the old man. There they would take out bushel loads of stock certificates that belonged to Armour's estate. Next morning

Andy would deliver these certificates to the brokerage houses through which Armour sold his shares. Armour then used the cash to support his long meat positions. Armour went broke and Andy wound up working at the Open Board.

One day, after getting whipped in the bean market, I asked Andy for a good stock to buy. His eyes lit up as he told me about an interesting railroad issue play. Yes, Andy was a professional at railroad recapitalizations. Railroads, Andy reasoned, had many assets, and they go bankrupt all the time. He bought issues of railroads that went bankrupt and waited for the reorganization courts to distribute their assets.

This was the 1970s, and the country's largest railroad, Penn Central, had gone into receivership. It was just coming out of receivership. Andy was right on top of this play. He called me aside and said there was a Canadian railroad company that held a lot of old Penn Central stock. This stock was going to be called back by the reorganized Penn Central. In its place the new Penn Central would give new Penn Central stock, which the Canadian government would tax at an exorbitant rate. Before this could happen Andy expected the railroad to sell out the Penn Central stock. It would then distribute cash as an extraordinary dividend. The old stockholders didn't get much for their money. The new stockholders were able to buy the former assets at a fraction of the cost of the older issues.

Andy expected the dividend to amount to $40 per share even though the price of the railroad was only at $38 per share. I looked at him in disbelief and said, "Come on, Andy. Isn't the market price going to adjust to reflect this?" He tried to convince me that the railroad, Canadian Southern Railway, had that exact play in mind, but I didn't think it would happen.

Andy looked at me as if I had given away a winning million dollar lottery ticket. He asked me to buy an odd lot if I had no interest in buying round lots. I thanked him politely and said that I didn't have the money available to take advantage of this particular play.

Four weeks later, the specialist suspended trading in the stock because the company announced a special dividend of about $40 per share. The stock went from $40 to $80 per share overnight. No one could find Andy the next several days.

I became ill thinking that I could have doubled my money in four weeks. I could have bought the stock on margin and tripled my investments. Here was good fortune staring me in the eye and I asked it for credentials!

As the week went by I found the lining to my stomach and put the antacid tablets away. I went to Andy and told him that he was right. He asked if I had bought any stock. Grimacing in pain, I told him that I had not. He bought early and heavily, hinting that he made over $200,000 on the play.

This is not the moral nor the end of this story. It is only the setup to the following sequel. Several months later I asked Andy if he had another play that could make so much money so fast. He paused to think it over and then said that he had tracked another stock that would be a very big money-maker.

My mouth salivating, my stomach acid churning, my heart palpitating, I waited for Andy to give me the details. He said, "It looks like the old Peoria & Eastern Railway will get a good settlement on the Penn Central bankruptcy. Yep, you gotta buy Peoria & Eastern." I listened intently as he explained the details of the play. The Penn Central railway had rented feeder tracks that belonged to the Peoria & Eastern Railway. Penn Central wasn't paying the lease fees for the feeder tracks because of the bankruptcy. The move out of bankruptcy meant that Penn Central would make all the accrued lease payments to the Peoria & Eastern Railway. Stockholders and bondholders would benefit. It looked like another winner.

To garner more confidence in the play I asked Andy how much he was going to buy. He was so confident that he planned to buy not only the stock, but also the bonds. Penn Central had made no payments to its bondholders since the bankruptcy. With such enthusiasm emanating from his face, I just had to buy the stock.

I took money out of my trading account and bought several hundred shares. I bought at around $19 per share . . . all the way down to $14 per share. I was very bullish on this play. I even convinced a building contractor who was doing some work at our family business to buy 2,000 shares for his own account. Of course, I couldn't have convinced the contractor if I hadn't told him about the double-your-money-in-one-month play. We both looked at the play as another Canadian Southern Railway dividend play.

I bought and I waited . . . and waited . . . and waited. One month went by . . . two months . . . three months. I went over to Andy's corner after the market closed one day to discuss the Peoria & Eastern Railway stock play. Yes, Andy was still long. He was still buying. He asked if I had bought any for my account this time, and I proudly announced that I was long several hundred shares.

Meanwhile, I found lucrative trading opportunities at the Chicago Board of Trade. I moved away from the Mid-America Commodity Exchange and lost touch with Andy. I would see him on LaSalle Street once in a while and I would ask if he knew anything about Peoria & Eastern Railway. Yes, he was still long and he was still buying.

Months turned into years. One year turned into two years, then another year. Three years had passed since I first bought the stock.

I watched the stock and tracked the bankruptcy court hearings. It was a thinly traded stock, so I had to read the pink sheets weekly. I even called up the only over-the-counter market maker in Peoria & Eastern stock to get price quotes. I showed up at all the Peoria & Eastern

Railway annual meetings. My contractor friend, meanwhile, passed away. During one of the annual meetings I met his widow. We sat together on one side of the conference table along with another stockholder who wanted us to join him in a class action suit. Opposite us were the lawyers representing the Peoria & Eastern Railway company and Penn Central. I found it strange that the same lawyers were representing both railways. Year after year the lawyers told the stockholders the same thing: Rewards come to those who wait.

I checked the stock like an intern monitoring a patient on a life-support system. I had expected a quick one-month play, but this one would eventually span my trading career at three different exchanges. As I think about it now, I wonder why I didn't ever unload the stock. At one point it went down to $9 per share. Andy said he was long and was still buying. Would I doubt him a second time?

Three years turned into four, then five, then six, then seven. By this time I had forgotten about the company and the stock. Penn Central suddenly announced that all parties had agreed on a final settlement. For each share of Peoria & Eastern stock, Penn Central gave the stockholders $27 in cash and about a one-third share of new Penn Central stock. Penn Central stock eventually went up to around $70 a share.

I went to the bank vault to take out my Peoria & Eastern Railway certificates. I had them broken into units of ten shares each when I took delivery seven years earlier. As I look back at the reasoning I remembered how wildly bullish I was on this play. I expected to be able to sell these odd lot certificates in bits and pieces for huge amounts of money.

This reasoning wasn't to be. The markets did not repeat the first dividend play that doubled the price of Canadian Southern Railway in one month. The second play lasted seven years, but the money invested, around $15 per share, went to over $75 per share. The knowledge I gained by analyzing the stock over seven years and by dealing with lawyers and company presidents was very helpful to me as a stock market investor. I learned over the seven years of tracking the stock that it took time to make money in the markets. A get-rich-overnight stock had captured my interest and lured me into a long-term position because the fundamentals looked very good. This experience taught me the difference between trading for a living and investing for a profit. The difference is patience.

At the time I was learning this lesson, I traded in and out of stocks frequently. I got in one day and got out the next day. I bought Columbia Pictures at $2.25 per share and sold it for up to $7 per share. (Coca Cola bought a big piece of it years later at about $70 per share.) I bought Allied Products at $6 and sold it at $7. (It eventually got up to $34 per share.) As Peoria & Eastern forced me to hang on, my own trading strategy got me to trade in and out all the time. While my investment account was generating a 30 percent annual return, I was looking to make a few points in my trading account.

Patience is indeed the hardest part of trading and investing, but also the most important. We can study books and attend conferences on how to become better traders and investors, but it is in the waiting that we make bigger profits. This lesson taught me to buy Ralston Purina at 10½. I still own it. It traded as high as 92. I bought Tandy at 24. Now for every share I bought, I have four shares trading at 42.

No one can teach you patience in the markets. You are your own teacher in this regard.

RULE 15

Sell Short as Often as You Go Long

This rule was formulated years ago, but it is somewhat inaccurate. It should state: "Be willing to go short as well as long, but not as often." This modification implies that markets go up as well as down, so if you are to be a professional trader you must be amenable to shorting the markets also.

The original rule suggested that you should go short as often as you go long. That is, if you are long for five trades, then you should also be short for five trades. This is not the case because markets do not spend an equal amount of time being bullish as being bearish. In fact, it takes the markets more time to go up than to go down. Given the same amount of price movement on the upside as on the downside, the markets will take about three times as long to accomplish an up move as a down move.

There are several strategies for accumulating a position, based on the types of markets you are trading.

The first case is that of a grinding, up market. This is classified as a bull market. Since it goes up very slowly and methodically, you can buy a portion of your commitment at selected spots and accumulate more stocks or futures as prices continue to improve.

When you liquidate positions towards the top of the bull move, you should sell out your total commitment. Unless the futures or stock has a wide sponsorship with very good depth, the distribution at the top will often be short-lived, so get out and take your profits quickly. If the stock or futures has wide commitment and support, then you can take your positions off in a series of trades.

At the top of the market, the strategy for initiating short positions is defined by the way the market behaves at high price levels. Since price does not stay high for long, you should short your total commitment in one block. Once the move to the downside occurs, you will not have the opportunity to short more stocks or futures. If you are not already positioned for a downward move, you will have to chase prices down if you want to initiate short positions. Unlike an upwardly grinding market where you have ample opportunity to buy at your pricing, the crashing downside market will not provide you with opportunities to accumulate short positions.

Scalpers in the pits are attuned to the types of markets they are trading in. In grinding intermediate trends to the upside, intermediate and long-term traders can pick up contracts here and there. These slowly grinding up markets push the patience of the scalpers to its limits. The scalpers thrive on quick market action, and when they buy something at a low price, they want to sell it immediately. In bull markets, the scalpers, who are trading with much smaller amounts of capital, make money with great agony. Eventually, the prices will move up, but they have to hold on to their positions for three times longer than they are used to. When they are holding on to a position for a longer time period, they are exposing themselves to greater market fluctuation risks.

In downward markets, on the other hand, scalpers make a lot of money very fast. They sell short towards the top and, in about one-third the time it takes them to nurse a profitable upside position, they make the same amount of profits per trade in downward moves.

The amount of money that was lost in the one day crash on October 19, 1987, far surpassed the miniscule amount of money that was made by the scalpers on the downside. Outside traders, who were not trading with a short-term scalper's mentality, but from longer perspectives, lost hundreds of millions of dollars, while certain scalpers were known to have made $5 million.

I personally like to short bear markets more than I like to go long in bull markets, and I like to do so with a longer time frame. This is not because I have a scalper's mentality. I look beyond what is currently happening with my shorts and see market opportunities after I have unwound my bull market positions and before I institute my bear market positions.

Envision this scenario: The stock market is at the bottom of a long bear market that has spanned several years. I buy certain blue-chip stocks. Then the market goes up and prices become inflated. I add to my positions. After a while, I want to take my profits, independent of what I think the market will do. I unload my stocks and with my profits I look around to buy secondary issues that have not appreciated as much as the blue chips. I know that I can accumulate these at relatively bargain price levels. I ride these stocks to the top of their moves and then shift to the tertiary stocks. After I unload the tertiary stocks, practically everything is still high priced and inflated. I now find that the universe of bargain stocks has diminished. If I moved away from stocks, I could park my money in money market funds or other instruments that will pay me to hold their investments.

The following scenario of selling in bear markets is more to my liking: I have no positions and I see the markets topping out. The stock prices are overvalued, and one by one each leading issue rotates from distribution into weakness. I short a few stocks here and there. Individual issues start to crack and, in their first sell-offs, they drop dramatically. After the initial collapse, they come back to test their previous highs; then they start the slow, agonizing move downwards. I continue to short on the way down. When I am at the bottom of the price move, I cover all my shorts. With my profits securely stashed away, I look to go long on some real bargains. Not the relative bargains that I had to look for when I was at the top of the bull move, but real undervalued assets of major companies. There are real bargains at this stage of the market's move. Stocks that were selling at $60 at the top can now be bought for $6 per share.

My buying power for stocks is ten times greater at the bottom than at the top. This is the secret to successfully playing the short side. Not because I can make money fast, but because I can buy real bargains at the bear market's bottom with the money I made from the short side. For the sum of $25,000, I could have bought a controlling interest in the whole RCA company at the bottom of the stock market in 1932. At the top of the market in 1929, $25,000 would have bought an odd lot. Who knows what opportunities await the bear market buyers at the end of our current bull market?

As a general rule, selling short as often as going long is not effective because the markets don't stay at the top as long as they stay at the bottom. However, you should be willing to sell as well as buy.

RULE 16

Don't Buy Something
Because It Is Low Priced

This rule, like most of the others, is valid when applied to the right market situation. The question is, How or when do you know you shouldn't buy at low prices, or sell at high prices?

There have been many cases where a stock price went to all-time lows and then went lower. There have also been as many cases where the price went down and then abruptly reversed to start a major bull move. What is low and what is high?

As much as I would like to say that I have some rules of thumb for determining "low" and "high," there is really no way to conclude from price activity alone that prices are low or high enough to accumulate or distribute stocks. To evaluate whether low is low or high is high you need to look at several aspects of market accumulation, price action, and time cycles.

In the cases of IBM, illustrated in Figure 16–1, and Elcor as shown in Figure 16–2 there were intensive accu-

Figure 16–1. **Daily chart of IBM stock and on-balance-volume indicator, August 1986 through March 1987. Courtesy of Equis International's Metastock professional software.**

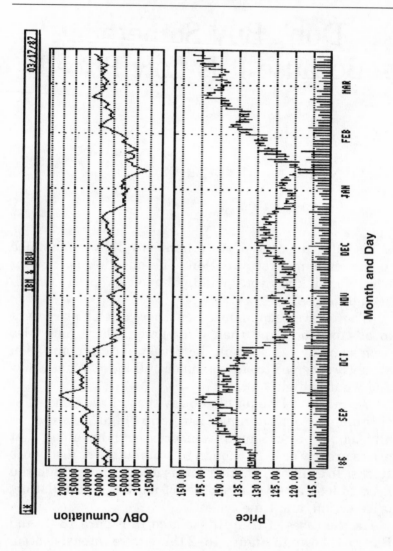

Figure 16–2. **Daily chart of Elcor and on-balance-volume indicator, January 1986 through April 1987. Courtesy of Equis International's Metastock professional software.**

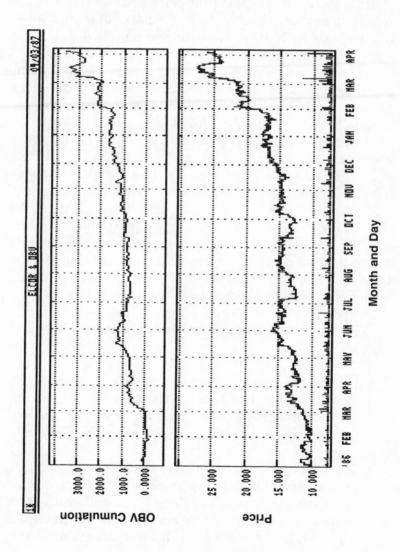

mulations as shown by On-Balance-Volume analyses at the low end of the price range.

In the case of Allied, Figure 16–3, the distribution pattern at the high prices showed topping action, but it still went higher!

It is foolish to assume that price activity alone is the sole indicator of whether or not a particular market is low enough or high enough to warrant investment or speculation. On the contrary, it is important to look at other indicators to help you make a more refined interpretation of market action. You can make your decisions to buy or sell based on volume and time-cycle activity, or a combination of all three indicators.

Unfortunately, the market is evaluated on price activity alone: the net price change from a previous period. You won't ever hear your margin clerk say that you will have to get out of your positions because record volume of stocks traded this morning. In the same manner, the clerk is not likely to want you out of a position because today is the second year's anniversary of the previous high. These indicators, however, are critical in helping you determine what low is and what high is, yet nobody in the business uses these indicators to the degree that they use price indicators.

The following points should help you assess lows and highs.

- Look at long-term price charts to obtain a perspective of where price has been in the past. Is the current price at historical lows or highs? If so, the chances are very good that the current lows or highs should hold.
- Try to put the correct phase of current action into perspective. Where is the market in relation to price sensitive indicators like long-term and short-term moving averages? If the markets are bullish, old highs probably won't hold. If the markets are bear-

Figure 16–3.   **Daily chart of Allied and on-balance-volume indicator, January 1986 through April 1987. Note that price drops a little in May and June, then hits a new high, then hits a new low. Courtesy of Equis International's Metastock professional software.**

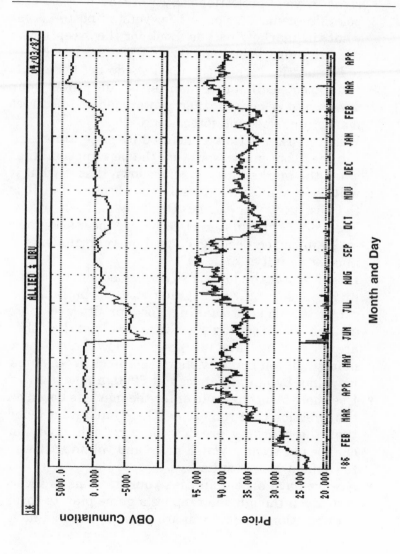

ish, old lows probably won't hold. Use Elliott Wave analysis to determine the stage of market action, and weekly or monthly charts to see where price has been. Learn how the various technical indicators are behaving in the current market phase.

- Try to project price activity. You do not have to be right in your projections. By working over several possible scenarios, you set up your mind to accept what the markets will do. Look for the exception to the rules also. When you do this, you are less likely to be surprised when the markets do not behave as you expected. If future market action proves your analysis to be correct, then you are closer to correct market analysis and forecasting.

- Watch market action as defined by price, time, and volume. You must work on the assumption that when the market does go up or down that is what it will do in the future. This is not absolute, but it is the best that you can do. Don't fight the markets. Your role, as speculator, is to observe the market and make informed decisions based on your analysis of market activity.

- Either buy at the lows, if so confirmed, or sell at the highs, if so confirmed. Otherwise, do nothing because the odds of making good profits are more against you in selling short into new lows than they are in buying into new highs. How much more money can you make by shorting a stock at $2, a new low, than by buying a stock at $200, a new high?

- Use short-term charts to enter the markets based on the direction that you decide. Once you have decided that the markets are low or are high, look for changes in trends. Watch price and volume activity to confirm your results.

- Always have an out in case your analysis is incorrect. Even though you prepare a game plan to cover your positions in case you are wrong, you must have correctly positioned yourself in the market to prevent catastrophic losses from inflicting permanent damage to your trading plan. A trading career is not made on one big trade, but on a series of profitable trades.

An interesting approach to buying low-priced stocks was used by John Templeton, chief investment officer of Templeton, Galbraith & Hansberger and Templeton Investment Counsel. Shortly after World War II John Templeton took an inheritance of $10,000 and invested it in stocks listed on the New York Stock Exchange. In a short article written about the great investing acumen of Templeton in *Forbes* magazine, Templeton disclosed that when he left the army in the 1940s he bought $10,000 worth of stocks trading at $1 or less listed on the New York Stock Exchange. His rationale was that the economy would be booming after the war ended and most companies would benefit from the increased business activities. Four years later, he sold out all his holdings and made a $30,000 profit.

Most of the stocks went down and even disappeared from listing on the New York Stock Exchange. The ones that did go down obviously sold below their previous lows. With these stocks, the lows didn't hold, yet Templeton saw beyond the lows made by these stocks. Through a mere probability approach he allowed the ones that made new highs off their lows to make substantial profits for him. When he was wrong, he lost only $1 per share. When he was right, he more than tripled his capital. These winners showed huge gains in his portfolio. The ones that did bounce off the lows rallied and made new highs.

He used common sense to create his initial investment success. How much farther down can a stock trading at $1 go? With "low" prices like these and a portfolio approach to diversify the risks, investment success was virtually guaranteed. He removed the necessity of precise timing, which is needed now in our current investment and speculative climate, by first analyzing the direction of the main trend, and then investing with that directional trend.

RULE 17

Pyramid Correctly, If at All

In order to trade profitably, you must take a position in the market so that you can make money if the price moves in your favor. But even if you are correct in your analysis of price movements you won't be able to parlay your profits into more profits unless you have a plan to increase your position. This is why traders pyramid: They need to increase the size of their commitments to make bigger profits. This is where Rule 17 comes into play.

Another way to make more profits is to increase the frequency of trading without increasing your positions. This strategy is contingent on two factors: cost of executions and price skids. The best place to implement this strategy is the exchange floor, where all orders from the public are centrally executed and price skids are minimal. Successful floor traders are those who can combine increased transaction size and increased trading frequency.

In order to add on to an initially profitable position so that you can take further advantage of a favorable price move you must have two prerequisites. The first is that the market you are positioning in must be moving at a slow enough pace that you can add more to your positions; the second is that the market must have a sustained, one-directional move.

In pyramiding you are looking for opportunities to add more positions with minimal risk to your total equity. Most successful pyramids have been created during massively bullish markets. Few speculators have been able to pyramid successfully during bear markets.

When you decide to pyramid in a market, you are looking for profits from initial positions to allow you to either margin or buy outright more positions as the move continues in your favor. In bull markets, the price moves to the upside are slower and more protracted both in time and price. In reactions in bull markets, prices drop suddenly but start to recover their losses just as quickly. Eventually prices reach new high levels. As the bull market unfolds, the speculator has the opportunity to buy more positions in the direction of the trend.

Pyramiding is not possible in bear markets because of the very nature of such markets. Bear markets go down fast and stay down. Reactions in bear markets, i.e. counter-trend up moves, are quick and brief. These reactions are quick to the upside because nervous shorts are rapidly covering their positions. These bear market reactions are brief in price stability because trapped longs are rushing to break even by unloading their positions at the rapid price escalations.

In bear market pyramiding you are looking for weakly sustained price action that will allow you to go short at the prices you want. Bear markets do not provide price floors for the speculator to sell additional positions within a reasonable amount of time. In most cases, before more short positions can be created the prices would have dropped.

There are also certain market-specific biases that make pyramiding difficult. In the United States stock markets, the person who shorts must sell short only on either upticks or equal ticks from the previous price. The short seller cannot sell on downticks. This in itself limits the possibility of the short seller entering shorts in bear markets moves if there are no upticks to allow the short seller to go short.

Secondly, the pyramid you build must be able to take advantage of a strong one-directional move. If there is no such move, then you will wind up just adding to a cumulating position at various prices that are close to your average price. There will be no price move that will cause your total position to appreciate in value. If a strong one-directional move does occur so fast that you have a limited opportunity to add on to your pyramid, you still will not have substantial profits accrued from previous positions.

A separate problem here is the ability to forecast when one-directional moves have the highest probability of occurring. This is a matter for fundamental and technical analysts and, in extreme cases, for astrologers and readers of tea leaves.

Mechanically adhering to pyramiding can make substantial profits if there are also sound rules to enter stop loss orders so that losses can be minimized. (See the stop loss orders, Rule 8 and Rule 33, to determine what price levels to use in placing stop orders.) The basic rule of pyramiding is never to allow any subsequent position that you add to the total position to get so large that if there is a retracement the total profits are wiped out when your stop loss order is executed.

When you decide to pyramid in your next campaign, you must decide whether you will add positions in equal or varying amounts. From my own experience I know that adding more positions but at lessening numbers is the correct way to approach pyramiding. Pyramiding in

93

equal amounts of contracts or shares can also produce surprisingly good profits, but this requires a bit more analysis.

There are basically three ways to pyramid your total positions: inverse, normal, and averaging to market. Averaging to market is not a strict pyramiding approach, but it is included here because all the approaches are conceptually the same: You add more positions to your total position so that you can take advantage of future price appreciation.

The inverted pyramid is the correct way to approach pyramiding. Your initial position must always be the largest position of all your total trades; as more positions are added, each successive addition must be smaller than the previous ones. The mechanics are as follows:

Purchase No.	At	Buy Shares	Cost	Average Price
1	$75	300	$22,500	$75.00
2	$80	150	12,000	$76.67
3	$85	75	6,375	$77.86
4	$90	35	3,150	$78.62
5	$95	25	2,375	$79.32
6	$100	15	1,500	$79.83
TOTAL		600	47,900	

As you can see, the number of shares added diminishes with the increasing market price. The average price of the total commitment stays close to the $75 level. As the market price increases, there is an increasing chance that the market is vulnerable for a price correction. The price correction of the market, if it truly is a bull market, will not, probability-wise, retrace close enough to the starting price of the move.

The second approach, that of pyramiding in equal amounts of shares, can also result in good profits. However, there is an inherent weakness in this normal pyramid relevant to the inverted pyramid, as illustrated below.

Purchase No.	At	Buy Shares	Cost	Average Price
1	$75	100	$7,500	$75.00
2	$80	100	$8,000	$77.50
3	$85	100	$8,500	$80.00
4	$90	100	$9,000	$82.50
5	$95	100	$9,500	$85.00
6	$100	100	$10,000	$87.50
TOTAL		600	52,500	

The inverted pyramid resulted in a total position of 600 shares with an average price of $79.83. Total cost of the 600 shares was $47,900. In the normal pyramid a total position of 600 shares was also accumulated, but at an average price that was higher than in the inverted pyramid. The average price was $87.50 per share and the total price commitment was $52,500. The average price of the normal pyramid was $7.67 higher per share, and the cost for the same number of shares was $4,600 more.

The capital risk of the inverted pyramid is all borne out in the initial positioning. In the inverted pyramid, the risk on the first purchase was three times greater than the normal pyramid, a $22,500 purchase versus a $7,500 purchase. In the second purchase, the cumulative risk was $34,500 ($22,500 + $12,000) versus $15,500 ($7,500 + $8,000) for the normal pyramid, or about two to one capital at risk.

It is only after the second purchase that the additional risk capital increments are in favor of the inverted pyramid. In the third purchase, the trader adds $6,375 of stocks in the inverted pyramid and $8,500 in the normal pyramid. The risk of adding capital now swings to the normal pyramid: a factor of 1.33 times. In the fourth purchase, the trader adds $3,150 to the inverted pyramid and $9,000 to the normal pyramid: now a factor of 2.85.

What you see here is that when one begins an inverted pyramid, the risks to the market campaign are up front. In the normal pyramid, the risks are spread out over the cumulation pyramid. From a strictly mathematical point of view the risks are evenly spread out over the normal pyramid; however, market reality impinges on this analysis.

The market was hypothesized to have moved from an initial low price of $75 a share to a high of $100 a share, a price appreciation of $25. If the market were to reach a high of $100 a share and retrace, we could theoretically pose three possible retracement prices: one-third, one-half, and a full two-thirds retracement.

With a $25 one-directional move without a sustained reaction, we can assume with a high probability that a one-third retracement will cause the market to bottom out at $91.67 [$100 − ($25×0.33)]; a half-way retracement would cause a bottoming action at $87.50 [$100 − ($25×0.50)]; a two-thirds retracement would cause a bottom at around the $83.33 level [$100 − ($25× 0.66)].

The average cumulated price for the inverted pyramid was $79.83 and for the normal pyramid was $87.50. The $79.83 price for the inverted pyramid is not within the two-thirds retracement price of the whole $25 move, whereas the $87.50 average price of the normal pyramid was reached on the second possible retracement scenario of one-half. With the average price of the normal pyramid, there is a two out of three chance that the retracement will force the trader out of his or her total positions at a slight profit (at $91.67 and at $87.50) and a one out of three chance with a breakeven or a slight loss (at or around the $87.50 level).

RULE 18

Decrease Your Trading After
a Series of Successes

I went over to the Chicago Board of Trade in the spring of 1976 when the exchange offered prospective members a deal in which the exchange financed the purchase of three types of trading permits that could be converted eventually to FIM memberships (financial instruments markets). The FIMs themselves were eventually converted to AMs (associate memberships). The three different types of permits allowed holders to trade one of three new or developing markets: commercial paper, gold, or Treasury bond futures. I was one of one hundred people who bought permits to trade bond futures and one of three hundred who bought the permit.

Among the group that entered the trading pit in futures that year was a guy by the name of Chuck Cohen. Chuck was my age, so we immediately hit it off. For the first year, Chuck struggled to learn the ropes of scalping in the pit. He traded in small lots and as the bond futures markets grew in volume, he slowly found himself being edged out of the trades. He was wired all the time and would respond to each trade like a jack rabbit darting out of the closing teeth of an animal trap. At the close of each trading day, his jacket would be wet with sweat. Yet, he usually wound up breaking even during the course of the day. Every so often he would make ten or twenty ticks a day for his profits—usually the result of several hundred trades. Chuck earned his money.

One day, Chuck and I sat down to compare notes. He had a great trading day and had made over 30 ticks in bonds, or about $650. He was very proud of himself, and I was very proud of him. It is very hard to make money in trading.

We all hoped Chuck would succeed as a scalper, despite the fact that other traders, including his friends and colleagues, were profiting from his mistakes. In fact, the mentality in the trading pit is similar to that of the water buffalo in the South African plains who are under attack by lions and tigers. When they know that they are about to be attacked, they gather together in a circle and face outward with their heads lowered and their horns directed at the attackers. The buffalo know that they must form in this manner for the safety and protection of themselves and the others. In a group they can thwart all enemies; alone they fall prey to the superior claws and teeth of the lions and tigers.

In a similar manner, all traders know that their own financial viability depends on the soundness of other traders. They know that when they trade with the other person in the pit, that person must be able to honor that trade. They also know that if they lose money, they will lose it to the other traders or brokers. Yet, they all must stand together in the pit against the outsiders. The individual trader doesn't want to lose, yet he or she wishes that the other traders would also win. They look up to those who succeed against the terrible odds for success.

A strange environment to work under, indeed.

One day Chuck had made a considerable amount of money before the day was half over. I suggested that if he was running such a good streak, he should go back in to trade for the rest of the day. He said, "No way, Bill. I'm going home to take a nice long bath. I deserve it." He disappeared for the rest of the day.

Later in the year, I talked to Chuck when he was on a losing streak. He continued to trade, despite the fact that he was losing. He didn't want to be beat by the markets, yet he wound up losing even more.

Chuck did exactly the opposite of what a successful trader does. When he was winning, he whimsically stopped trading. When he lost money, he continued to trade instead of taking a break.

There are trends in one's life, just as there are trends in the markets. When you are young and in college, you can go out drinking at night and be ready to attend classes the next morning. When you are old, you need to rest, and even a small amount of alcohol will cause you discomfort the next morning. Go with the trend at the time. If you are trading and you are a winner there is no reason why the trend must stop. The trend is for you to follow; most people think that if they stopped trading with the trend, the trend will stop. Trade until you encounter losers, then stop. When you experience a string of losses, stop and come back again. Don't try to hammer the markets.

In the same manner that you must know when to stop trading and take a rest, you must also change your trading style at different stages of your life. When you are young and your reflexes are razor sharp, you can be a good scalper. You can turn around at the drop of a hat and hit the bids and take out the offers before anybody else. When you approach middle age, your joints start to hurt if you stand in the pits longer than half a day. You flex your knees often and yawn when the markets become quiet. At this stage, you progress to longer term trading. When you are old, you position trade. This diminishes the capital risk that you take on and hence your level of stress.

These observations on the life cycle of a trader are based on the "rule of three tens," which I learned from David Goldberg, the founding partner at Goldberg Brothers. This rule points up how long it takes to become successful in the futures trading business. It divides a trader's career into three ten-year blocks of time.

You spend the first ten years on the floor scalping and making a living. You make money one day and lose it the next. Over the course of ten years you learn to make more than you lose, you learn the ins and outs of the business, and you gain the ability to scalp for a living. During the second ten years you really start to make money. Hopefully, all the lessons you learned in the first ten years are producing a consistent and solid income for you. During the second decade you must make enough money for the third. During the third decade you use the money you have made in the second to make more money. At the end of the third decade you should be retired from trading and making money from your investments.

This rule presents an expected time frame to learn the business, to trade the markets, and to retire. If you try to modify the market's sequential ordering, you will encounter nothing but frustrations. You must do what the markets want to do.

In the case of the rule of three tens, you know what one can and must do at different stages in life. But when the markets are trending, how do you know if the markets are set to reverse or will continue onwards? The simplest rule is that if you are having a string of winners, don't stop trading haphazardly. Using the simplest definition of a trend reversal—when you have a string of losers—then you stop. If you stop trading because you have had a string of winners and think that the odds are that the string will end soon you are trying to impose your will on the market. Let the market tell you when to stop, and that is at the slightest hint of a trend reversal.

RULE 19

Don't Formulate New Opinions During Market Hours

Successful trading requires many strong talents, and one of them is planning the trade. You must view the execution of a trade as part of a whole-brained approach, a gestalt.

When I was actively trading several years ago, I did most of my market analysis after the close. I would formulate a trading strategy for the next day and list the markets that I had to watch. When I placed my orders to enter the markets, I had a plan of entry and a plan of exit. If the markets behaved according to my scenario, I would hold the trade. If they behaved differently, I would sit back and observe their behavior. I had already established a strategy to get out of the markets if my analyses were wrong.

Most traders spend all their time figuring out what to do in the markets. They never give much thought as to what they would do if their analysis was wrong, much less what they would do with the trade if it was profitable.

This is the main reason they lose money in the markets. If the markets don't behave according to their half-hatched trading strategy, they grab at anything—ideas from their brokers or what they read in the *Wall Street Journal* that morning. This information will serve as the crux of their new trading strategy.

In January 1989, the market traded in a range of 2,200 at the high end and 1,900 at the low end and had been in that trading range for the last year. A friend of mine had a strategy to sell at the high end of the range and buy at the low end. Premium sellers of calls and puts were raking in the money. My friend called me and told me that he had bought a bearish put spread with the Dow industrials at around the 2,175 level. He planned to leg off one side of the put spread when the market dropped. He actually had two positions on. He would liquidate one side of one spread and hang on to the other spread position as a single position. If the market went up from there, the amount of money that he paid for the spread would be the most he would lose. His total risk was known up-front.

The market dropped about 100 points, and he saw his spread widen in his favor. Up to this point, his strategy played out exactly as he expected it. After the market bottomed out at 2,080, it started a move upwards and broke through previous highs at around the 2,206 level. At this point, my friend had planned to hold onto his position and watch the spread erode to the maximum loss. That was the original game plan. Instead of legging off one side of one spread when the price dropped, he legged off one side of the spread at the new high level of the Dow industrials. This was his first mistake.

He might try to rationalize his mistake by saying that his strategy was incomplete, but I would disagree. He had a strategy if the market went down, and he had a strategy if the market went up. He just never executed a part of his plan. Call it a lack of discipline or whatever you

104

wish, but he never followed through on what he originally intended.

My friend might also argue that he saw new data that he needed to input into his original strategy. I would say that if he designed the original strategy for a certain market scenario he should not tinker with that strategy if the scenario no longer held.

My friend had originally allowed for a $1,500 loss on two bear put spreads. Instead, he wound up with one $2,000 loss on one spread that he liquidated and a $1,000 loss on the second spread that he held. An original loss of $1,500 was doubled to a $3,000 loss.

The lesson in this example is not to change your original strategy. Instead, carry out a new strategy with a new set of approaches. If you analyzed the market originally to be bearish and designed positions that would take advantage of a bear market, you must continue through with that analysis. If the market conditions become more bullish, you cannot tamper with the original strategy. You must liquidate the strategy as originally planned, then redesign and reimplement a new strategy geared to the new market conditions. If you try to change your strategy during the trading day based on new market action or new information, you probably won't have the full resources that you would normally have to help you make a more informed decision.

The correct approach is to analyze the markets first. Design a strategy or entry point where you want to position yourself in the markets. Plan where you will exit and where you will put trailing stop orders if your analysis is incorrect. Plan orders that will allow you to squeeze the market movement for maximum profits; then wait for the market to come to you.

I like to relate a story about Texas Slim, a professional gambler, because it shows how to approach the markets successfully. After one particularly grueling tournament that he won, a spectator in the audience went up to him and asked him to play a game of ping-pong for several hundred thousand dollars. Texas was a professional poker player, and he didn't know anything about table tennis, but the spectator finally talked him into playing the game with him. Texas obtained one concession: He would play with his own paddle. The spectator agreed, on the condition that he would play with the same paddle to equalize everything.

Texas practiced his ping-pong game day in and day out. When the day came for the match, he walked into the playing room, reached into his carrying bag, pulled out an empty pop bottle, and handed it to the spectator. Then he pulled out another empty bottle and told his opponent that he was ready to play. The empty bottles were the paddles!

Needless to say, the spectator lost, despite the fact that he was probably the best ping-pong player around. An unlikely paddle like pop bottles became the strongest tool that Texas could have used to win the game. He forced his opponent to play a game in which he did not know how to use the tools.

The markets are always forcing you, the unsuccessful speculator, to trade on their terms. What you must do is control your environment to the point that you take the risks that are on your side. There is no failure with adequate preparation. Those who fail in trading the markets fail because they don't know what to do with the tools that they have. The markets are erratic, and it is your role as a successful trader to isolate these random movements with your knowledge and experience so that you can predict market movements.

R U L E 2 0

Don't Follow the Crowd—They Are Usually Wrong

This original rule has been around so long that most people today immediately dismiss it as contrarian trading and investment psychology. Let me be a bit naive and ask: What is the trading crowd? Where is the crowd headed that I don't want to follow? Is the crowd ever right?

And if you are a crowd follower, you won't be able to run out the door at the same time as everyone else when someone says "Fire" on the trading floor. The problem that we all have about following or not following crowds, running out the door or staying inside, is that we don't know what the crowd is, or what running out or staying in entails.

When you decide to buy something, you don't want anybody to find out about your investment. Only after you have taken a position do you want the crowd to follow you and buy the same investment. With their later buying, you can sell to them if you need to, and their buying makes your holdings more valuable. You can buy at the same time as the crowd, but you won't make as much as you would have had you bought earlier. However, you cannot sell when the crowd is selling. Getting ahead of the crowd is very critical when you are selling.

With the current milieu of government agencies beefing up regulations and grey area trading by exchange members, you must be sure that you aren't in the position of influencing investors. If you want to tout your long positions, you can't write about it in your newsletter or tell your employees in the bank's trust department to buy. This is strictly prohibited in the interest of fairness.

Crowds can be right at times and can even cause markets to fool the professionals. Every so often, the crowds can wrest control of the markets away from insiders and professionals and give these players a run for their money. This is where the term "oversold bull" originates. When the markets go higher after your analysis has led you to take your profits, the markets can continue straight up and cause the most astute insiders to unload their holdings at market's new highs. The problem doesn't end here for the professionals. Most of the damage occurs when the market continues even higher. The professionals, having already gotten rid of their long positions, now institute a short selling program. (It's so difficult to buy again after you have made a substantial amount of money on a major position.)

The quandary posed to the professional when the public takes hold of the market applies not only to bull markets, but also to downside markets. Horror stories abounded after the October 19, 1987, worldwide market crash. Friday, October 16, was the first day of the massive downdraft. Many professionals who were still in business on that day told me that they had substantial profits on Friday's close. They came into the markets Monday opening short and made embarrassingly huge amounts of money immediately at the opening bell. As one professional told me: "I couldn't help myself. The market just handed me fistfuls of money." It was what happened during the rest of that Monday, October 19, that did these professionals in. The market opened much lower, rallied, and then sold off dramatically. On the opening, some pros covered shorts. As the market went lower, they started to go long at 150 points lower, then 200 points lower, then 300 points lower, then 400 points lower. It looked as if the lows of the century were going to be tested. At the bottom they sold all their positions.

I wouldn't say that this day was under *direct control* of the public—How can you say that one has control of one's body when hurtling over a cliff screaming, "I'm sure I will hit bottom!" The effects were the same, nonetheless. The public went over the cliff at the same time, and the professionals tried to support the falling bodies. Who was smarter? Public speculators and investors in the back pushed the public in the front into the chasm, all the while getting a bigger and bigger crowd to follow.

When I first started to trade grains at the Mid-America Commodity Exchange in 1972, I saw soybeans go from $4 a bushel to well over $12 in July deliveries. Wheat prices topped out around the $6 level and corn went up to $4 a bushel. The highs of the soybean markets of 1972–1973 haven't been surpassed even as of this writing. In the process of doing this, the markets fooled the professionals, and many floor traders lost their shirts. Prior to this massive bull move, the highs in the beans were around $5 per bushel.

Around the first new highs, professionals went short by selling the front months and buying the back months—they created bear market spreads. As beans went higher, the spreads first went to even money. The price of the front-end beans contract was exactly the same price as a future delivery contract months later. There was a pressing demand for beans at the here and now. As the bull market continued, the difference between front-end beans and back-end beans became greater still.

The beans for delivery here and now traded well over the prices of beans for future deliveries. Because of the demand for the cash beans and the lack of available beans for delivery, the short sellers of outright positions and the biased short bear spread sellers found themselves caught in a squeeze. The bean shortage eventually reflected in the all-time high of $12.90 per bushel for July 1972 beans. The move from $6 to $12.90 meant a profit of $34,500 per contract of 5,000 bushels of beans. The bearish short seller did not see the spread move exactly that amount, but the July/November 1972 (old crop versus new crop) bean spread went from a 25-cent premium to $4.90 per bushel premium on the front month, or $23,250 per contract. Public speculators profited at the expense of the professionals. The masses were able to cash out to big numbers in this move.

The gold (Figure 20–2) and silver (Figure 20–3) markets were wildly bullish in 1979 and culminated in a high of about $800 for gold and $50 for silver. During the up move, everybody who had been hoarding gold and silver for the past decade cashed out. In the meantime, the professionals on the floor were heavily short and sustained tremendous losses.

These examples of specific cases where the public was able to take control of the markets from the professionals are stellar. Such cases make the headlines but don't make money consistently. Unfortunately, such occurrences are rare. In the last 20 years, only a handful of such publicly controlled markets have existed. Meanwhile, had you played along with the professionals, you would have made a substantial amount of money. As an outside participant with limited risks, you are in the unique position of being able to capitalize on most of these stellar moves.

Figure 20–1.   **Monthly continuation chart of soybean contract traded at Chicago Board of Trade, 1968–1988. Courtesy of Computrac software, version 2.8.**

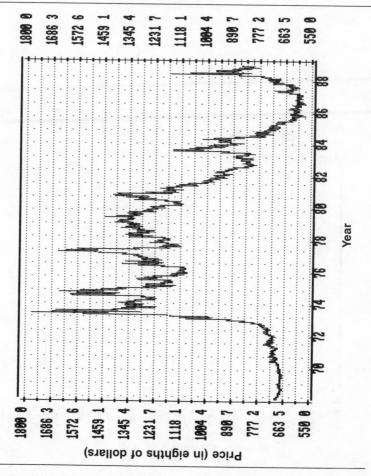

Generally, the public loses money in most markets. Don't allow a few cases where the public has made money to influence you to take sides against professionals all the time. In the long run, my money has always been on the side of the professionals.

Figure 20–2.   **Monthly continuation chart of gold contract traded at Commodity Exchange, 1975–1988. Courtesy of Computrac software, version 2.8.**

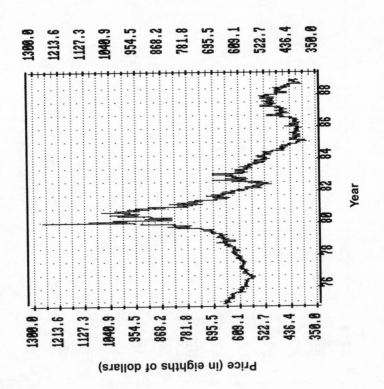

Figure 20–3. **Monthly continuation chart of silver contract trade at Commodity Exchange, 1971–1988. Courtesy of Computrac software, version 2.8.**

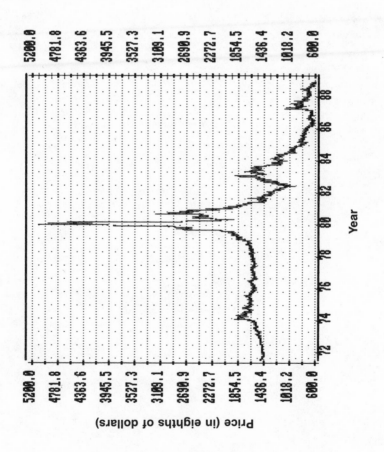

RULE 21

Don't Watch or Trade Too Many Markets at Once

A remarkable salesman told me years ago that the human mind is a wonderful thing: It can process millions of thoughts at the same time. Unfortunately, because of the limits of the five senses, only one or two of these thoughts can be externalized at any point in time. He likened it to trying to fill an empty bottle by pouring water into it through a funnel. The water accumulates at the funnel's top, but it still has to drop slowly through the opening at the bottom. Try as you might, if you pour water into the funnel at a faster rate, the water will not go through any faster than the bottom of the funnel will allow.

The same can be said for trading many markets. The fact that there are more than 6,000 stocks, an infinite series of options on those stocks, more than 50 futures contracts and an infinite series of options on those futures, ever-expanding debt instruments, and so on, ad absurdum, offers you, the trader or investor, a myriad of speculative and investing opportunities.

When I started trading, I had lots of time but no capital. I thought then that capital placed an absolute limitation on trading opportunities. Now that I am in my forties, I have lots of capital, lots of opportunities, but no time.

The amount of capital that you can use to play in the markets does limit the number of issues you can track. If you have a lot of money, you can trade a lot of markets. If you have a small amount of capital, you have to become more of a money manager than a manager of positions. When the unseasoned trader looks at any market with a keen eye for margin leverage, the door is open for abuses of capital management. The question then is, What do you do with the capital you have, and how do you do it?

If you took the easy way out and placed all your capital into one investment, then you could watch it diligently. But is this the best way? Isn't there a more effective way of investing a fixed amount of investable or tradeable funds by increasing the number of markets or instruments that we invest in? The other approach is to go to the extreme and buy a few contracts here, a few of another there, until all the investable funds are thoroughly diluted among 20 or 30 investment or speculative vehicles.

Peter Lynch, the funds manager for the Fidelity Funds, is so spread out that he is invested in several thousand stocks. The mass of his investable capital is so large that he can't stay in the area of stocks and remain a successful money manager. Several years ago, a money manager for the Prudential Insurance company said that he could no longer invest in stocks because he had so much money. He said that if he were to shift to the stock area completely, he would be able to buy the capitalization of the New York Stock Exchange blue chips several times over and still have money left over.

Jack Gaumnitz, while he was working on his doctorate degree at Stanford University in 1967, studied the diversification of risk in a portfolio of securities. He discovered that once the number of securities in a portfolio reached 18, risk could no longer be lowered effectively through diversification. Another doctoral student at the University of Washington, John Evans, discovered in 1968 that five randomly selected securities in a portfolio proved to be as risky as 2,400 tested portfolios with one to sixty randomly selected issues. Evans diversified by investing equal dollar amounts in a given number of stocks; in other words, if he started with $50,000 as a portfolio, he would create portfolios of five randomly selected stocks with $10,000 invested in each, all the way to sixty randomly selected stocks with $833.33 invested in each. The conclusion reached by Chris Mader and Robert Hagin, authors of *The Dow Jones-Irwin Guide to Common Stocks,* 1976, was that "a typical portfolio with equal dollar amounts in just five stocks, selected for diverse risk characteristics, will have only slightly more risk than would be attained by placing equal dollar amounts in all stocks." Therefore, it isn't necessary to track all the markets, nor is it necessary to trade only one closely watched market in order to diversify your risk and limit exposure of capital.

Their experiences might not be directly applicable to you, but you do have the resources nowadays to track historical price action, forecast future price movements, and monitor news activity of a greatly increased number of stocks, futures, or options. With the advent of computer technology, what took several hours to do manually years ago can now be done instantaneously.

I tracked the markets that I traded and diligently charted their price and volume activity every day. When I went on the floor to trade, I narrowed the time interval from daily to hourly, then from hourly to every quarter hour, and finally from quarter hour to trade by trade. My tracking of market action by driving down the time interval got so ridiculous that at any one point I had more than 15 tick by tick charts in my trading jacket pocket. There were the tick by tick charts, the three-minute bar charts, the fifteen-minute bar charts, the hourly bar charts, the half-hour bar charts of the cash markets, the daily spread chart of the front-end contract versus the back-end, the daily charts of the major indices, the moving average charts, the oscillator charts, the relative strength charts with several different time durations, etc. Then there was the reports almanac I carried around in my vest pocket. It stuck out so I could easily look down to see what reports were being issued today, the next day, the next week, next month, even compare numbers from a year ago. The monster that I created got out of hand. The fun of trading got lost in the mounds of charts and reports I was tracking.

As traders are wont to do, I treated the problem of information overload by throwing money at it. I reasoned that if there was so much information available, so many ways to massage that information, so many markets to trade, so many derivative products from those markets, so many ways to do so many different things, it was certainly necessary to study these. I looked at the many tools available to study these many things.

The next thing I knew, I had computer overload. There were the Sphere, the Altair, the Imsai, the Apple, the Radio Shack, the Tandy, the Macintosh, the IBM PC, the clone, and the clone's clone. With these came the software packages to manage the miniaturized behemoths of computing power. The Dow Jones Stock Analyzer, Meta-Stock, Lotus, Window on Wall Street, Breakout and Outbreak Systems, the Technician's Toolchest, Options Analyzer, Optionvue, SideView, and End to End. In effect, to be a minimal survivalist in this ever-changing market, I had to be a specialist in computer hardware, software, trading strategies, and money management.

Everybody can use technical analysis but most don't understand it yet. There is a void of understanding. The

118

existence of computers has created a strange paradox of understanding. On the one hand, the computer software and hardware used in trading makes it much easier to trade: In a span of a few milliseconds, the trader can analyze one market. In a span of ten minutes, the world of investment analysis is at his feet. On the other hand, the average public investor doesn't know how to use these tools, which were once the province of heavy-duty money managers and sophisticated traders. Unless he or she has actually worked with these techniques, the average investor will be at a loss as to how to use them to trade the markets effectively.

Computerized trading technology has created a wealth of opportunities for money managers, but it also has bifurcated market participants: We now have people who manage funds and people who have funds to be managed. Fewer and fewer people know how to manage money well, while the number of people who have funds to be managed and are computer illiterate is increasing. As in the other areas touched by computers, the gulf between those who know and those who don't know is becoming wider.

As in all cases where technology overruns itself, computers can only benefit those who already know what they're doing. The object of computers is to free up your time so that you can analyze a market with more precision, not to free you to analyze more markets. I think it is a good idea to go back and work some charts by hand once in a while to get the feel of the price action. There is something to be said for actually seeing patterns unfold when you add them to a chart. It's like going back to nature to get your bearings.

R U L E 2 2

Buy the Rumor, Sell the Fact

Please note that the statement is to *sell* the fact, not *buy* the fact. Implicit in this rule is the assumption that the rumor is bullish. Rumors, however, can as easily be bearish.

Bullish rumors are what you base your buying on. Once the bullish fact is known, then it is too late to buy because the bullish news will have been factored into the market price. Instead, it should be sold. The idea, then, is to buy in anticipation of bullish news and sell when the news is out.

If the rumor your hear is bearish, leading to actual bearish news, then the statement, buy the rumor and sell the fact, does not hold. In fact, there is a greater danger to your trading equity if you buy on bearish rumors and sell on bearish news. Markets have a tendency to go down a lot further and a lot faster than they go up. With this action, it would be foolish to establish a long position in anticipation of a bearish rumor becoming fact.

121

To establish a short position in anticipation of covering the short when a bearish rumor turns to fact is a better strategy, but not by much. The risk with this strategy is great. First of all, you don't know what the market has already discounted before the rumor becomes fact. This problem is inherent in all rumors. Secondly, there is a chance, slim though might it be, that the market you are interested in might even rally on the bearish rumor becoming fact. This would be attributable to the fact that the established shorts would use the bearish news as an opportunity to pull in their shorts.

If I have confused my readers with all of the above scenarios, I only want to illustrate the difficulty in trading based on rumors. I do absolutely nothing with rumors, and I watch very carefully when the facts come out.

How do you distinguish facts from rumors? The key is the source. Facts come from known and reliable sources such as government or corporate reports. The sources of rumors are unknown, so their validity is suspect. Rumors are created in the minds of traders who are trying to account for unknown causes of price and volume activities. If enough rumors are created around these observed price and volume activities, a few of the rumors will actually justify the heretofore unaccountable market action. When facts are offered, then the connection is made between these "valid" rumors and the facts.

The intelligent trader acts on the price action alone, with a keen eye on volume activity. If there is activity without facts, then something is going on, and it would be wise to close out positions by selling out longs or covering shorts. Only when the rumors actually become fact is it safe to reenter the market.

For the same reason I caution against entering positions in anticipation of government reports or other facts. Before any government reporting agencies make their announcements, the wise trader closes out all positions and waits till the markets reopen with the news already factored into the price and volume action. If the trend that existed prior to the announcement is resumed, then it becomes that much stronger. If the announcement is contrary to the previous market trend, the trader has an opportunity to watch a substantial test of the trend's underlying strength or weakness. Trends that are in force take time to reverse, so if someone is positioned in the direction of the main trend, and that trend is veritably killed by news announcements, that trader still has a very good chance to get out at a slight loss.

Initiating any positions prior to the news announcements is gambling. If you are wired to some government insiders and have access to information before the public obtains it, I urge you not to use that information in your trading. The immediate profits you make will certainly cause the governing agencies to look at your trading records. With the current regulatory environment on the nation's commodities and options exchanges, it would be foolish to jeopardize a lucrative profession for an inside trader's profits.

We all need hopes and dreams to give meaning to our lives, but wishful thinking can cause tremendous overstaying of positions. Wishful thinking comes about after a position has been instituted and the facts are already out, seldom before.

RULE 23

Take Windfall Profits When
You Get Them

In the course of your trading career, there will be situations that offer you spectacular profits without your having to exert much effort. For instance, assume that the stock of a small company that you are long is suspended from trading one morning. Later, the company announces that a larger company is tendering for stock at double what its closing price was. This is a windfall profit. The same would be true if you were long a financial futures contract and the Federal Reserve announced before the opening that it had lowered the discount rate. All interest rate futures contracts would open up the limit.

For most people, windfall profits are good. Because prices in these situations appreciate so rapidly, people don't have the chance to limit their profits by selling out too soon. They can't help but make money.

Unexpected, spectacular losses are similar to windfall profits in that investors and traders have no control over their investment environment. The difference is in how the traders respond. In the case of windfall profits, I seldom see traders add to their winners; instead, they cash out immediately. There have, however, been documented cases of traders adding to their dramatic losers by buying more or selling more short.

A personal friend and trader on the Chicago Board Options Exchange told me about a situation that he handled correctly. He was completely bearish on the stock market beginning with the first new highs of 1987. He sold every new high by creating call and put option positions that would explode into profitability overnight if the market dropped dramatically. And if the market continued to make new highs, his spreads would break even and he would only be out on the commissions. For months he continued to break even on his options spread plays. He is an extremely disciplined trader.

The market topped out in the summer of 1987, but it did not crack suddenly. It started a grinding move downwards for about two months. This type of move did not make any money for my friend. Because of the way he designed his spreads, he was losing money on his positions because of the slow, grinding premium erosions.

In October of 1987 he found himself in a situation that called upon all his years of experience. When the market started its downward move on Friday, October 16, his spread positions started to make money. On Monday, October 19, the market opened lower and went dramatically lower that afternoon. As he saw the market trade more, his spreads behaved differently from his original game plan. Premiums on puts that he was short exploded. Call premiums, on the other hand, did not drop dramatically, which they should have done to reflect the continuing drop in the major stock indices. He had a situation in which the puts that he was long rose rapidly, the puts that he was short rose rapidly, the calls that he was short didn't budge, and the calls that he was long dropped slowly.

Profits that accrued to his account on Friday were gone by late Monday morning. In the early afternoon, after marking his position to market prices, he saw that he was down another $280,000. The money lost in the morning came from his unrealized profits. The money lost in the afternoon came out of his pocket. Logic indicated that all the options were mispriced according to all the valuation models. They were grossly overvalued because another pricing model had been instilled into the options premiums: the fear model of option valuation.

As he related to me months later, he could sense the fear on the floor. No market maker was willing to step up with the other side of a public order without first extracting exorbitant premiums. All the market makers wanted to make back their losses; some were so deep in the hole that they had to make it back on one trade.

As the market approached the closing bell, my friend made a very difficult decision. He had managed to stop the equity hemorrhaging in his trading account. Now, he had to remove the malignant tumor. He checked his positions and isolated each option series into total numbers of positions. He walked into the first crowd of market makers and asked for two-sided markets. The anonymous crowd responded. He took out their offers and hit their bids. One hundred of the 50 strikes, 150 of the 75 strikes. On and on. He repeated this in every crowd of market makers that he had options spread positions in.

By the closing bell, he had whittled his options positions down to zero. His account equity had dropped from $650,000, which was the preopening valuation, to $225,000 after the crash.

He had planned on the market going down, but not that far. The market dropped so low and pushed his spread positions so far beyond his parameters for profitability that his original game plan failed. In this regard, he was in the same boat as all the other market makers. What started out as a substantial profit situation turned into an unexpected and large loss.

As my friend related to me at the end of the year, the original positions that he had going into that morning of the 19th of October showed substantial mark-to-market losses. However, had he kept all those positions, even with the mark-to-market losses, he would have wound up making well over $500,000 at the first expiration of some of the options and another $175,000 at the end of the second expiration on his remaining positions.

My friend's decision to close out his positions was not profitable. Had the situation turned into one in which his designed short spread positions were capable of making profits on the dramatic drop, he would have taken the windfall profit by liquidating his positions.

As a professional, he had designed his initial play to take advantage of a market drop. The drop occurred, yet instead of making money, he sustained more losses. Instead of waiting for the markets to settle, he did what a trained professional does: He played the market when he had control of it.

He no longer had control of the market, and he had illogical losses as a result of it. Instead of trying to salvage the situation, which could have been done under better conditions, he unwound all his positions. He then sat out the rest of the unfolding scenario while the market action waited for the premiums to play catch up. I do not suggest that if you have a planned scenario and design positions around this scenario that you attempt to change your strategy in midstream if the scenario does not unfold. In the case of my friend, he played as well as he could, but it still wasn't enough. What more was there to do, even with his years of experience, than to close out all positions and wait?

In order to take advantage of windfall profits, or any profits that may come your way, you must first have some minimal game plan—not something that you follow like an automaton—but a guide to help you plan for contingencies that often arise in trading. If you expect a certain minimum level of profits, not a maximum profit objective, you should have no trouble figuring out what to do if the unexpected occurs.

There are markets in the current state of price action that offer profits on an overnight basis. The currency markets have always done so. Most profits in currencies are made by carrying positions overnight into the next day's gap openings. Markets such as these, which lack fluid price movements, tend to be dominated by professionals. As the public withdraws from certain markets, this kind of price action predominates.

In the currencies you will find that overnight windfall profits and unexpected losses are the rules rather than the exceptions. Once the gap opening has been made, market prices probably won't continue to trade in ranges wide enough to afford day trading profits. In these particular markets, it is wiser to ring the cash register by taking your profits.

Other markets such as the highly liquid Treasury bond futures contracts, are very high volume and can afford day trading profits. The gap openings are less likely with such markets. Here, the strategy is entirely different. You only have to look at intraday analysis techniques to make good profits.

R U L E   2 4

Keep Charts Current

This rule used to be the bane of professional traders because most charts were done manually by the individual traders themselves. They would spend hours updating the markets, only to find that they had only a few hours left before the market would reopen and they would have to analyze it all over again. Of course, with these limitations on time, only a selected number of markets could be tracked. The average independent trader tracked about ten in a portfolio. Anything more than that required computers and various charting techniques.

With the advent of personal computers, I found it much easier to maintain the small number of stocks and futures I was tracking. However, as many of us do when we have implemented a time-saving device or service, I went overboard by picking up more things to do with these new aids. When I was trading off-floor, I found myself tracking about 15 markets simply because I had more computer resources available to my trading.

As a floor trader I could track only a few markets, such as soybeans and T-bonds. When the markets closed at 3 P.M. central time, my daily analysis just started. I would wait a couple of hours for the prices to be made available on the computer dial-up services. During that time I would busy myself with odds and ends of work. I would set up the computer to do the automatic run routines. The machine would dial into the database, retrieve the data for that day, disconnect from the database, and wait until I got back to attend to it.

Oftentimes I would come back from dinner and move the files around on the computer storage device. The computer then would create the new charts and spend the next three hours creating hard copy charts. At around 9 or 10 in the evening the charts would be finished. I would take a break to watch the 10 o'clock news and then spend the next two hours studying the charts; if I saw anything interesting, I would spend another hour or so doing additional research.

There are quite a few charting services—Commodity Perspective, Commodity Trend Service, Financial Charts, to name a few. These services are a convenience for those who don't have the time to update their charts, but because these charts are prepackaged and sent to you on a weekly or monthly basis, I don't think they give you a good feel for the markets you are trying to trade. My instinct as a trader is that I must rely on myself.

Another problem with the weekly charting services charts is that you have to update your charts manually during the week. With a computer, you can load the current day's data into your files and create a new chart with the updated pricing. Of course, if you make extensive notes on your charts, you can't readily transfer them onto the next day's computer printed charts. In this case, I staple the original chart with my notes to the newly printed computer charts. This preserves my valuable notes and saves me the drudgery of updating the old charts. In cases where I have extensive trendlines and curves on the old chart, I will merely make a photocopy of it and add blank sections of graph paper to continue the chart. I don't lose the accuracy of the trendlines.

Another problem with charting services is the fact that there are no customized studies. If the publication follows a 14-day relative strength study (RSI), that's all you get. There are times when, if you had the data in a computer, you could change the relative strength line by shortening or lengthening the duration. I have a few pet studies I monitor that are not available on preprinted charts. When I study and see some interesting market action, I go back to the computer and output the charts with a different set of parameters. Instead of having looked at a 5-day moving average crossing over a 13-day moving average, I might want to see how a 14-day moving average crosses a 34-day moving average. I can't do this with the commercial charts.

The main advantage that the commercial charting services offer is cost. A weekly chart book of about 60 futures contracts runs about $10, or $40 a month. On a subscription basis, the cost is even less. If you were to update these charts with a computer and a software charting package, your costs would be three times that of the commercial charting service. It would take about four hours a day to update the files and get hard copy charts. If you are a broker and markets analysis is secondary to your role of soliciting business, you might want to use commercial charts, as long as you aren't trying to analyze the markets correctly for your clients.

Charts give you a frame of reference for market action. Any type of tracking, minimal though it might be, will give you a reference for future market action. If you do not track market price action through charts you could track price ranges. This is what Jesse Livermore did. He used charts, but what was more important for him was the breakout of trading ranges. He used these to track the upper range of prices and the lower range of prices to determine price limits.

A case can be made for manually updating the charts. With all the computerized power at our fingertips nowadays, it is nice to get a feel for the old days by manually inscribing bar chart lines on the chart pages. However, with the type of mathematical analysis that technical analysis so easily lends itself to, it would be difficult first to calculate these studies and then to plot them on the chart paper.

In the 1910s and 1920s technical analysis centered on tape reading tactics. Professional traders were capable tape readers. As more markets and more accurate technical analytical techniques came along, tape reading was slowly pushed aside by the more accurate momentum studies. With the advent of computers in the 1950s institutions created more advanced technical analysis techniques. Finally, with the creation of the relatively inexpensive, number-crunching personal computers in the late 1970s, a whole new world of technical analysis was opened to the public.

A systematic approach to updating your charts will also create discipline for you. If you do get software that allows you to update your daily charts on a nightly basis, set up a different schedule for weekends. Weekends are fraught with perils. I would often party on Friday night and forget to update my charts until Sunday night. A better schedule would have been to update the charts Friday night and then analyze them on Sunday night to refresh my strategies.

RULE 25

Preserve Your Capital

In an environment outside of trading, the above statement has great impact. The amount of capital that you have determines how successfully you can extend your very existence from the present to the future. With capital, you can invest in properties and companies that have future growth implications. Without capital, you live for the present.

The same holds true for trading accounts and trading careers. If you have the accumulated capital you have control over your trading opportunities and your career development. Conversely, if you lack the trading capital then you cannot control your trading opportunities and career.

There are many ways to control the risk to which you expose your capital, but there is only one way to preserve capital: by thinking out your trading situation and determining where the risk to your capital lies.

Most traders are very intelligent. In fact, trading and speculation appeal to white-collar professionals with above average intelligence. Many retirees trade in the markets often. With their years of experience in life, they have more wisdom to draw upon than the younger traders. Yet, these very same people often wind up with no money in their trading accounts after a few trades. How does this happen?

Many of us suffer from what floor traders call the "King Kong Effect." We think that the next trade is the one Kahuna that will make the year. Instead, like King Kong, who fell to his death at the height of his glory, we often end up losing everything.

I lost a substantial portion of my trading account when I was learning how to trade bonds. I thought this play was a shoo-in. The bonds opened lower that morning. My scenario called for a quick reversal to the upside. I had $10,000 in my trading account. The margin at the time was $1,500 per bond contract. Over the course of the years I learned the importance of controlling the exposure of my trading capital. As the market traded that morning, I initiated my first trade with two contracts. I say "initiated" because I eventually bought more contracts. At the time of the trade, I never expected to add more.

As the morning wore on, the bonds failed to show any signs of strength. In fact, they moved lower, to below my first purchase price. I reasoned that I could not safely buy more than six bond futures because of the margin requirements—six contracts at a margin of $1,500 per contract required $9,000 to control. As the price dipped lower, I bought two more contracts. Now, I was long four contracts at an average price that was higher than the current market price.

I was not alarmed that the bonds didn't show any strength right then, but as the morning passed and the afternoon began, the bonds still failed to show any signs of strength. I again positioned an additional two contracts at new low prices. Now I was long six contracts in a market that looked like it might rally, once, to let me out of my total positions. The old bromide that markets do not go straight up or down, but trade in racheting up and down moves, came to my mind. I tantalized myself into believing that I was going to be given an opportunity to get out of all my positions at a slight profit.

Unknown to me at the time was the fact that my starting capital base of $10,000 was rapidly eroding. I acquired my total six contracts at lower and lower prices. The last lot was the one that had the price closest to the market price, i.e. that showed the smallest amount of loss or profit (in this case, loss) from the market price. The earliest position showed the greatest loss.

Because I was a day trader trading with a short time frame in mind, I wasn't aware of the erosion of my trading capital—the capital I use to maintain a position in the markets. What started out as $10,000 for two contracts was now $10,000 less the mark-to-market losses, and six contracts.

At $10,000 and two losing contracts, I had a lot of room to run around in. At $6,000, which was the current mark-to-market equity, I had three times my original position. Anyone could easily see that with my $6,000 I was trying to control six contracts. Margin, strangely enough, remained at $1,500 per contract. In the morning I had $10,000, two positions, and a wish. On the close, I had six contracts, $6,000, and an unanswered prayer. I sold all my positions on the close at big losses. I wound up with $4,000 in my trading account and no positions.

My trading equity eroded due to market losses resulting from increasing positions. I was getting nailed at both ends. First, my total position in bonds was getting more costly relative to current market value. Second, the equity that I needed to sustain these and other trading positions was diminishing rapidly. The market losses based on the increased positions hurt, but not as much as the trading ramifications from those losses. With diminished capital as a result of increased bad positions, I had to trade smaller contracts and work the remaining capital much harder to get my trading equity back to $10,000. This is why many people are more successful trading from a deficit account than with a positive equity account.

Now, as a seasoned trader, I look back and know exactly what I did wrong. Losses are a given in the trading business. However, uncontrolled losses due to bad position management can cause debilitating financial and career damage. The example of my trading bind shows that even a professional trader with a well-planned strategy can get caught up in the trading game.

In ending this chapter, my suggestion is that you first control all the risks to your trading equity; then worry about how high the Empire State Building is. See Rule 21 for more discussion of how to control these risks.

R U L E 2 6

Nothing New Ever Occurs in the Markets

History repeats itself. So what else is new? What's new is that the *manner* in which history repeats itself is of significance in attempting to forecast future events.

Most speculators are too tied into the markets to see the stages of the markets they are in. They cannot see similarities in different situations, and they cannot extrapolate what they have observed into other situations. Markets are always repeating, in some form or another, what occurred in the past. But because the actual suggestions and implications are different, market players often overlook what they saw in the past and close their minds to nuances that can be important to a correct analysis of the current situation.

Creativity is important in the forecasting process because it helps you use previous situations to form another possible scenario. In thinking about how current conditions reflect what transpired in the past, it is necessary to know that not everything will be repeated exactly. Certain conditions will repeat, but others will not; some new conditions might come to the forefront.

In forecasting future events, there are three time brackets to consider: past, present, and future. It is beyond the scope of this chapter to discuss random walk and how it relates to market prices. Depending upon the time span of your analysis, it is possible to accept the random walk theory and at the same time to accept trending markets. If your market action analysis is based on a defined time span, and if you lengthen the time span, you will see the validity of the random walk theory, but if you define your time frame to be progressively more discrete time intervals, you will see that you can forecast imminent price moves.

There are two types of thinkers who are active in the markets: forward thinkers and backward thinkers. Each group has its strengths, but only one excels in current markets.

Forward thinkers take past events and actions, input current actions, and arrive at a prospective scenario for the future. They use the backdrop of past events and current action to create an outline on which future forecasts can be fleshed out.

Backward thinkers also take past action, input new action, and look for past scenarios to repeat in the future. However, backward thinkers, as the name implies, are forever looking backwards. They do not add that extra consciousness in their thinking to accommodate more varied future projections.

For the last decade or so, many doomsday economists have been forecasting their own brands of Armageddon. I must admit that I once advocated a cleansing of the world's economic machinery through inflation-depression cycles, which were highly touted, both in the West and the Soviet East, but I was not as extreme as most modern day survivalists.

To illustrate how the critical differences in thinking can lead to incorrect analysis, I've analyzed past events centered on the Great Depression.

The economic conditions of the world back in the 1930s were dramatically different from today's. In the 1930s there was a developing steel industry and a new automobile manufacturing industry that was a consolidation of many smaller manufacturers. The United States economy was not nearly as deep as it is now. Now, the automobile industry itself generates enough gross annual sales to match the gross national product of a lesser developed country. The construction industry is so pervasive in the economy that it is a virtual lumbering giant with such bulk that it takes a long time for it to stop completely or start up again. Each sector of the construction industry can stand by itself and can represent a huge proportion of a smaller country's yearly budgetary expense.

Because the different sectors of the United States economy are so huge in absolute numbers, the momentum needed to get each sector going after a standstill or to cause it to come to a standstill is great. In the 1930s it didn't take much for the stock market to collapse. (This is not to say that there weren't aspects of the overheated stock market back then that made it vulnerable to a major collapse, such as indiscriminant short selling and futures-type margining of stocks.) Since the depth of the economy back then was so superficial, it didn't take long for the economy to collapse after the bulwark stock market dropped.

Today, margin requirements in the stock market are considerably higher, and short selling occurs only on upticks. Even though recent innovations such as standardized options trading on exchanges have circumvented the short selling limitations of the stock market itself, there are other safeguards built into the system that prevent the wholesale collapse of individual sectors of the economy.

141

What is unfolding now is that there has been a depression, of sorts, that has affected the United States economy. Each sector of the economy has taken its respective hit. Since the late 1970s there has been drastic downsizing of various sectors of the economy. The steel industry, which once employed more than 500,000 workers in the mid 1950s saw drastic downsizing and a series of industry shakeouts. At the nadir of the industry's depression, we saw United States Steel Company, once the premier world producer of steel, move out of the steel industry and become an energy producer. Now, the steel industry employs about 50,000 workers in the United States. With a leaner industry, any upturn in business translates into record profits.

In the automobile industry, we recently saw record earnings from Chrysler and Ford Motors. Before that, we saw depressed conditions cause Chrysler to downsize when it sold its tank division and cut back drastically on plant expansions, American Motors to seek a European partner, and Ford Motors to invest heavily in capital plant expansions. Monolithic General Motors has had extremely good sales, but it is a monolith. The depression that hit the automobile industry forced major repositioning of key players.

In the construction industry, we saw commercial and residential properties top out in the late 1970s. Since then, after the rolling series of depression-like conditions affecting it, real estate has been making selective rallies. The single-family home markets have moved to new high prices, aided by government policies primarily through the retention of tax deductions and the removal of tax shelters in commercial properties. In most areas of the United States, commercial properties have not regained their previous highs. The government knows that its bread and butter comes from taxpayers, so it has maintained the residential mortgage interest deductions.

Throughout the 10 to 15 years during which we saw such gyrations in the individual sectors, the United States economy found support in other sectors that had bottomed out earlier or were on intermediate rallies.

What we saw over the last 15 years can be classified as a "rolling depression." The depression of the 1930s was an *individualized* depression. In the 1930s, your neighbor got laid off. The depression of the 1980s and 1990s is an *institutionalized* depression. In the 1980s, whole sectors of the economy get work stoppages. Back in the 1930s home mortgages did not allow continual amortizations of the principal. Interest payments were made; and, at the end of the mortgage life, a lump sum for the equity of the home was paid. In the 1980s, monthly home payments include an amortization of principal, small though it might be. Today, lending institutions are feeling the squeeze even more than homeowners.

RULE 27

Money Cannot Be Made Every Day from the Markets

When I first started out as a trader at the MidAmerica Commodity Exchange, I made money on a very erratic basis. One day I would make several hundred dollars and the next I would lose several hundred dollars. On balance, I made a positive amount of money, but it was difficult to know what the accounting period was. If the accounting period was monthly, then I would have streaks of months where I made money and streaks where I lost money. This made for an extremely erratic cash flow, yet the expenses were steady and unrelenting.

The problem was compounded by the fact that the prior job I had was at the First National Bank of Chicago in the early 1970s. I was still living at home and had been spoiled by a steady paycheck. The monthly equation was always balanced:

$$Income = Expenses + Savings.$$

As a single person with no obligations, any money I made, I saved or invested in stocks. Before starting my independent career as a floor trader, I had accumulated enough savings to acquire a MidAm membership at $4,600 and to open a trading account for $3,000. As I devoted more time to futures trading, I learned to adjust to erratic income. It took several years for me to realize that the few markets I traded did not present profit situations every day.

There are three types of members and three basic types of trading they can participate in:

- Scalping members—scalp for minimum ticks
- Day trading members—day trade for intermediate moves
- Long-term trading members—position for long-term moves

Most members switch back and forth in trading styles, but outside traders can only use day trading and long-term trading with any effectiveness. The factors that affect the availability of trading styles are commission costs and ease of executions.

SCALPING DAILY FOR PROFITS

All scalping is done in one market at one point in time. I have seldom found successful scalpers in more than one market during a trading day.

A member of the exchange incurs relatively light commission costs. As of this writing, a member of the Chicago Board of Trade, when executing for his or her own account, pays about $1.50 for a roundturn commission and about 25 cents in additional fees and charges. For a roundturn trade, the member pays less than $2. If the roundturn is done at the same price, it is considered a scratch trade and the commission is merely 10 cents.

A minimum tick in financial futures contracts is $31.25. If the scalper makes a tick profit on one scalp, he or she can afford to make about 312 scratch trades and still wind up at breakeven for the day. As long as the minimum tick is considerably greater than the cost of a roundturn commission, the member who is a scalper can make a decent living scalping for minimum ticks.

Scalpers on the floor have extremely high commission bills. A friend who scalps at the Chicago Board Options Exchange has paid as much as $30,000 a month for member's commissions. The clearing firms prize these clients very much. Around Christmas time, they sometimes make their gratitude known by giving such clients $20,000 Cadillacs. Several clearing firms have condominiums in Hawaii, Florida, and Colorado available for the use of these members.

As members, scalpers are shown the public orders coming into the pit. They can take advantage of this information in the process of scalping into tick profit or loss situations. During a single trading session, the scalper can take positions in as many as 10,000 contracts, always looking to make a tick profit at best, a tick loss at worst, or a scratch at a breakeven.

Unfortunately, I am inclined to be a thinker. I found out early in my career that scalping offered a steady income, but it was a lot of work. Laziness was not the problem; I just felt more comfortable thinking out my plays rather than sweating for tick profits by trading 2,000 contracts every day. This attitude has not endeared me to the clearing firms. I remember telling the principal of a firm that I had made $700 on a 1-lot of bond futures. He didn't seem happy because his firm only made $2 on my trade.

Members who scalp have four basic advantages over the market and the retail public: 1) No capital is required to hold overnight positions, when dramatic news can move markets adversely against the trader. 2) Liquidity in the pits as public orders come in allows members to enter and exit the market with minimum losses. 3) Commission costs are less than the minimum ticks in all traded markets. 4) Scalping requires no real market analysis.

Scalping is not economically possible for nonmembers, largely because of commission costs. If a retail trader is charged in excess of $50 for a roundturn commission, that trader cannot break even on a scratch trade. A retail trader loses money on a scratch as well as a loss, can only make money if the trade is a winner, and has to have a series of tick scalp winners to make consistent money.

If the commissions were brought down to less than the minimum tick, retail traders would have a better chance of making profits, but that's not a chance I would take. If a retail trader uses the services of a discount brokerage firm that charges about $20 for a roundturn execution and the trader makes a tick profit ($31.25 in the case of bond futures), he or she winds up with a net profit of $11.25 less other fees. The retail trader can now afford to scratch only 0.5625 times on the next series of trade ($11.25 profit divided by $20), which is impossible since fractions of trades cannot be executed. Note that the retail trader can scratch only 0.5625 times, whereas in a similar tick profit situation, the scalping member can afford to scratch 312 times. The member has a 555 times advantage: 312/0.5625.

DAY TRADING FOR PROFITS

Once you move away from scalping, you will have a better chance to make money on a consistent basis, if you know how to create and handle your own risk opportunities.

If the market you are trading has a relatively large daily range, it is possible to day trade it for a profit, but not necessarily on a daily basis. Commissions are a serious disadvantage to the retail trader. In the case of the scalper we saw a member of the exchange who was as willing to take a tick loss as to take a tick profit. A day trading retail trader is willing to take many ticks profits as well as many ticks losses; he or she tries to minimize the losses while squeezing as many ticks as possible on the profit side.

Since the day trader, whether a member or an outside trader, is willing to take many more ticks losses to assure that he or she is in a position to take many more ticks profits, the capital needed to sustain these plays must be greater than a scalper's capital. The increased capital is required not because the traders will be carrying positions overnight, but because they are positioning during the course of the day. Once traders start to lengthen the time frame of their market risk, more capital is required to insure against market risk. In the case of the scalper, there was practically no long-term market risk: The scalper was out of the position on the next trade and in on another position on the next one.

Even with this increased potential to make larger profits, there is no assured way to obtain daily profits as a day trader. However, the scene is now set so that retail traders have increasing advantages over the scalping floor members. What was once a slight advantage to floor scalpers—that they scalp daily in only one market to maximize liquidity and centralization of orders—now proves to be a tremendous disadvantage if they try to day trade. Because the retail traders are not tied to one market in making their trades, they can watch several markets and trade opportunities that present themselves on a daily basis.

It is possible for the retail trader to make money on a daily basis in a few markets from a portfolio of many markets that he is trading. There is still no guarantee, but the chances of making money are better. Unfortunately, along with increased opportunities for profitable daily day trading also comes the potential to position into losing situations due to poor market analysis. The losing plays can offset the winners. Again, you have to be careful about trying to generate money daily, even if you are watching more markets.

LONG-TERM TRADING FOR PROFITS

As we lengthen the time frame for trading, we are discovering that the advantage of exchange membership is the ability to scalp markets. If the markets you are trading have enough daily movements over the range, then it can be profitable to trade on a daily basis if there are enough such opportunities. To increase such opportunities, you must track more markets.

Of the three types of traders we have defined so far, long-term traders have the greatest control of market risks. Because they take the longest viewpoint of market movement, these traders have the greatest number of profitable market situations available to them. The scalper has access to the orders going into the pit, but when the volume in that market diminishes, so does the scalper's advantage.

Long-term traders must also have the greatest capital base to work from. Since their approach is to find profitable situations and position themselves for expected moves, long-term traders do not trade every day as a scalper or a day trader with a large portfolio would. Rather, they accumulate large positions for longer duration moves. This means they need enough capital to cover margins and margin calls as a result of temporary setbacks and to cover their living expenses while waiting for the profitable moves to unfold.

The long-term trading approach is the most amenable to retail traders in terms of risk exposure, assuming that they have the capital to sit with losing positions for a long time. However, the long-term trader of such proportions is often a member of the exchanges. In order to take such huge positions, a long-term trader has to specialize in a few markets. An expert in such markets would find it advantageous to be a member of an exchange.

Professional traders know that they cannot make money every day. The money they make today could be lost tomorrow, so they adjust their expenses to accommodate erratic income flows. All traders recognize an inherent weakness with trading for profits: If you don't trade you don't make money. Hence, it is incumbent on the traders to trade every day. However, this isn't the way to make profits. Instead, traders should trade more on profit opportunities.

RULE 28

Back Your Opinions with Cash When They Are Confirmed by Market Action

There are several ways to enter the markets and make money. You can either play the market for a one-directional move and look to get on board a move when it does occur; or you can anticipate a move and position yourself ahead of time for this type of market action. Depending on the capital and resources you have on hand, you can implement strategies to take advantage of either of these scenarios.

Anticipatory markets are ones that you position ahead of time. Heavily capitalized traders and investors trade markets in this manner because they have resources that are not available to smaller investors and speculators. One such resource is research to allow them to analyze and anticipate ultimate trend reversals. Another resource they have is enough capital to position well ahead of an ultimate trend reversal. However, one of the ironies of having so much capital is the fact that they must anticipate market reversals.

The fact that markets can trade in units ranging from one contract to several thousand contracts shows that both small and large traders are playing the markets. Small traders have different needs and different advantages than larger traders. Small traders have no liquidity problem in most markets because they do not trade positions large enough to affect price movements to any extent. Larger traders, on the other hand, have enough capital that if they position themselves in one stock or commodity, they can actually move the price against the intermediate trend.

The difference between a small trader and a large one was shown to me many years ago by Harold Goodman, a very successful trader at the MidAmerica Commodity Exchange.

One day I was trading silver in the pit, and my analysis showed a bullish scenario. In bull markets, the strategy was to buy the breakouts to the upside. The first day I saw the markets go through new highs, I immediately bought several contracts. The problem with my strategy was that I was buying the breakouts to the upside all the time only to see the prices back off to somewhere around the middle of the previous trading range. As a scalper I sat with a long position in a bull market retracement. Because I was not heavily capitalized, I couldn't stay with the losses, so I managed to sell out at the bottom of the reaction. I continued to do this for several weeks, always sustaining losses.

Finally, I gave up and sat back away from the pit area just watching the markets make new highs. What was the problem with my approach? I was long in a bull market that was making new highs, yet I always got kicked out of my positions on retracements.

I went back into the pit and started buying breakouts on new highs; again and again I got hurt. One day I looked over and saw Harold Goodman walking into the pit. This was the first time I had ever seen him trading silver. I watched how he traded. He did the same things I did. When I bought a new high, he would buy on new highs also. In my case I only bought a few contracts, whereas Harold was buying hundreds. Day after day, Harold would talk about the money he made with his position from the previous day. In my case, I lost money day after day by executing the same trading strategy.

After losing a good chunk of my equity, I finally asked Harold what he was doing that was making him so much money. I bought when he bought, yet I had lost a lot of money doing exactly what he was doing. He leaned over to me and whispered that the difference between his position and my position was that he was already long in silver when he bid up the new highs. At the new highs he was only *adding to* his total position, which was partially obtained at much lower prices. He pointed out that I was right in being long, as anyone should be in bull markets, but that I was initiating *new* positions at the probable immediate highs of the moves. At the beginning of the day's trading, I was flat.

The difference between my trading and Harold's is like the difference between a large speculator and a small one. Harold was able to add to positions that he had already in place. In my case, I should have traded more on anticipation than actual breakouts because of the lack of capital in my account. Harold was playing for a longer-term perspective. He could afford to buy the new highs because he was only adding on to a larger total position.

RULE 29

Markets Are Never Wrong, Opinions Often Are

A young trader came to me one day to complain that the market had not behaved according to his expectations. He had positioned in anticipation of an extremely bullish government supply report. He went into the report long. When news reporting services announced the fully expected but diminished supplies, instead of going straight up, the market went straight down. My friend was puzzled at the market's reaction to the news, which appeared to be extremely bullish. He was several thousand dollars poorer and still naive about the markets.

This situation is repeated throughout the markets by all types of traders and investors. The basic problem is that they are unwilling to accept new market conditions or a new analysis of markets.

A similar problem arises when your broker tells you that she wants to buy a stock at $18 when it is currently trading at $25 because it is overvalued. She will wait until it dips down to $18 because that's what it is worth. Something is not right with this thinking. Or, in a situation where you are selling, you might be long a stock that is priced at $100 now. You decide that you don't want to sell it at $100 because you think it is worth $150 a share. Instead, you place a limit order to sell it at $150, good till cancelled. There is a similar flaw with this thinking.

In the case of the stock waiting to be purchased at lower prices, you are assuming that the fundamental and technical situation will remain the same when the price of the stock goes down to your buying level. In the case of the stock waiting to be sold, you are assuming the same. However, there could be hidden reasons why market forces are moving the price of the stock lower or higher. When the price actually does go up or down to your expectations, there must be new conditions affecting the stock. It is all right to make a future decision based on past events in certain situations because there are no other ways to approach the problem (use of past chart patterns to project future price movements, for example), but to predetermine sell or buy levels based on current misvaluations is not a sound approach to investing.

The correct way to approach the buying situation would be as follows: If the price of the stock is now $25 and you think it is worth buying at $18, you should watch the stock now and do not place a limit order to buy at $18. Put a trailing buy stop order above the current market price. If the stock has enough strength to move above its current lows, which may or may not approach $18, then it is worth buying. Do not buy based on price, but on the strength of market action. You are buying to be long in a bullish stock; you are not buying to go long in a stock that is making relative new lows. If the stock can go to $18, would you really want to buy it? This thinking also holds for bullish stocks. You want to unload your holdings in weak stocks, not strong ones. If the stock has enough strength to go to new highs, it would be foolish to sell it because it probably has additional strength to make more new highs.

Market analysis involves taking a set of parameters that have worked in the past to forecast price moves and looking for similar conditions to make projections. One obvious indication that your analysis of certain markets is wrong is that you can't make money in those markets. If you are correct, aside from serendipitous situations, you will make money. My friend who played for a bullish move based on bullish news was correct in his analysis, but the markets proved him wrong. The bottom line did not show him a profit. Problems arise when the trader insists that his or her incorrect analysis will eventually be proven right.

The two most recent examples of market gurus who could not change their opinions once the markets moved against them are Joseph Granville and Robert Prechter. In the late 1970s Joseph Granville, a market technician who wrote a very popular newsletter, made a series of very good market calls. In 1979, his impact on the market was so great that, when he announced a reversal in the market, it promptly dropped. However, as the market's conditions changed, he got caught up in his own importance. What was once applicable because Joseph Granville had the only tools that called the market correctly for a number of years suddenly would not work. Instead of watching the markets to adjust for new conditions, Granville died with his analysis.

Robert Prechter is our most recent casualty as a market guru. For a number of years, his application of the arcane Elliott Wave theory correctly forecasted imminent price moves. However, as more of the public followed his analysis, the Elliott Wave theory became less precise. More accommodations to exceptions had to be made. Yet, while the markets changed, the applications of his approach did not. It is fine to have discovered a theory of market analysis that is stringent in its precepts, but the stringency in all market analysis is also its greatest weakness: it does not accommodate for changing market conditions.

In all fairness to my colleagues, I observed their problems develop years before they became popular with the investing and speculating public. As any technical analyst knows already, once you have the majority of the public follow your methods, those methods will no longer work with the precision that they once did. The market gurus were caught up in analyzing the markets for the public's need, not for what the markets were telling. This fault rests with the media's need to create gurus and experts for the eventual consumers, the investing and speculating public.

As analysts, Joseph Granville and Robert Prechter are superb. As traders bent on survival in the marketplace, they are failures. They failed to realize what all successful traders know: if you are losing money, you must get out of your positions first, then re-evaluate the situation. If you are a successful trader, you cannot subject yourself to the losses that their analyses created. Somewhere along the line you must stop and think for yourself. You are then freed to evaluate these gurus' opinions, and dispense with them if you wish, in order to do justice to yourself as a risk taker.

The market is the final arbiter of fundamental and technical analysis. Regardless of what we perceive as bullish or bearish news, the market will do what it wants to do.

R U L E 3 0

A Good Trade Is Profitable Right from the Start

How do you know that the trade you entered is a good one? When the trade starts to show a profit. When you buy a stock or futures contract, you are indicating that the price you are paying now is lower than what it will be at a later period.

During the course of the trading day, the price of your stock might fluctuate above and below what you paid for it. The momentary losses are noise inherent in any market action. Do you consider this noise to be a part of your profit analysis?

There is noise in all markets. The unfortunate problem in this day of computerized trading is that we can define more discrete time, price, and volume intervals. Years ago, we analyzed market action based on weekly and monthly charts; now we work with daily and hourly time intervals. As computing power increases, the intervals of market analysis can be reduced even further. We eventually will have the capacity to analyze market action in fractions of seconds. Along with the capacity to analyze market action based on more discrete intervals of analysis comes the problem of defining losses and profits.

When markets were analyzed using weekly and monthly charts, the risks given for each market situation were broader than they are now. If the price of a $30 stock traded in a $5 range on the weekly charts, market strategists allowed a risk factor of about $5, but seldom less. That is, they allowed the price to go against them by about $5 before they started to worry that their analysis might have been wrong. As the intervals of market analysis lessened to daily, the stock was found to have a $2 daily trading range, so the analysts would decrease the risk from $5 to $2. With each decreasing interval, the risk in each trade was reduced to reflect the decreasing range of prices.

The situation now allowed market analysts and traders to reduce their capital exposure by reducing the intervals of analysis. In the process, something was lost in the analysis of market action. Instead of seeing major trends developing in market movements, where a good portion of the money is made in speculation, traders now saw ticks. Instead of living for the long term, they traded for the short term.

With short-term analysis, the definition of profits and losses were correspondingly changed. Instead of looking for a $10 profit in a long-term stock trade, the trader looks for day trading profits of 25 cents in a quick scalp. The problem is that in reducing their intervals they forgot to adjust their losses to 25 cents per trade. Their losses remained at $10 per trade while their profits dipped to 25 cents per trade.

A practical approach would be to limit your risk exposure to the same level as your profit potential. If you trade long-term for $10 profits, make sure that your potential loss is no greater than $10. The ideal situation, however, would be a variation of this. If you trade long-term, do not limit your profits at all, but still maintain a $10 potential loss. In a more discrete time frame, if you want to trade for huge profits, do not limit your profits, but maintain a 25-cent potential loss.

Going back to the original rule of this chapter, where we minimally identified what losses should be relative to profit potentials, you will see that profitable trades always start out as winners and can wind up as losers, depending on the perspective you allot for the trade. Unprofitable trades may or may not start out as winners.

If a trade you put on shows an immediate loss, you either bought at the high of the move or you bought in a downtrending market. If your trade shows an immediate profit, either you bought on the low of the swing or else it had the strength to go up higher than where you bought it. In either case, the price will continue to move in your favor. A trade that initially shows a profit will have a tendency to continue to show a profit.

If you are a floor trader, then when it backs away and shows losses, you must look at the loss in the same frame of reference as your profits. If you are a day trader, the same caution holds: View the loss in the same dimension as your profit potentials.

RULE 31

As Long As a Market Is Acting Right, Don't Rush To Take Profits

Many times in my earlier years of trading I carried profitable positions for several days or weeks. Then suddenly, without warning, I got an "urge to purge" and liquidated all my profitable positions. I often had to cash out profitable positions to pay the rent, telephone bill, utility bills, or whatever was more pressing at the time. Regrets ensued when the positions I liquidated continued to make profits...for someone else.

Richard Dennis, trader extraordinaire, realized the need for capital to trade larger positions, so he cut his expenses to the bone by removing all need to spend profits. His close friends observed that when he had accumulated well over $500,000 in net worth in his early twenties, he still had not spent any money for a new pair of pants. Traders who visited his apartment in the early years observed that his living room had hardly any furniture except a stack of *Wall Street Journals*. Everybody sat on the papers or empty crates. The money he made in the markets he plowed back into the markets selectively, but with ever-increasing positions.

The market moves up with no regard for the size of your positions, so why not take advantage of it by positioning with right numbers suitable to your trading equity?

After my trading career progressed to the point where I was able to make a stable income, I found that I had conditioned myself with a wrong set of responses. My conditioning to cash out profitable situations to pay bills also carried over into trading situations when I no longer needed the profits to pay bills. I jumped at the chance to make a tick profit here and there because I had become so used to ringing the register in the past. What was once a correct response to the conditions I was living under was now inappropriate if I wanted to make huge capital gains. Like most unsuccessful traders, I had conditioned myself to the wrong actions. Cashing out early is never the right way to make huge capital gains.

As traders, we are constantly bombarded with situations that demand buy or sell decisions. If the decisions are right, we make money, if the decisions are wrong, we lose money, but we are never at a loss for decision-making opportunities. In fact, we thrive on the opportunity to make more decisions in one day than most people make in a month. It allows us a certain amount of control over our own destiny, microcosmic though it might be. However, we can't get carried away with the decision-making process. Scalping is the only trading role where continuous decision-making in the form of executing and closing hundreds of trades on a daily basis is a precondition for success.

The need to experience an adrenaline rush from putting on a trade is not a prerequisite to successful trading. If you are a floor trader and every trade is a physical confrontation with the enemy trader, you need the adrenaline to get you into the "fight or flight" response. These responses have served our ancestors well in their quest for survival. However, in the arena of speculation for profits, constant decision making does not make for successful trading. In fact, constant decision making and the risk arising from increasing frequencies of positions can even expose your trading equity to greater losses.

Think of it this way. When you buy something, you want it to go up. When you sell something, you want it to go down. The chance of entering the trade correctly is small, but the chance of exiting the trade correctly is smaller. The chance of being right on both entering and exiting is the smallest. With such diminishing odds of coming through with a completely correct and, therefore, profitable trading campaign, the fewer decisions you make in the markets, the more profitable your trading should be.

How many people actually get to sell at the top or buy at the bottom? At most, a handful in each reversal area. First, you must be a market follower, once the market has told you what it wants to do. If the market is a raging bull, you have no alternative but to buy. If it is bearish, you have no alternative but to sell every time you get the opportunity. Let the market tell you what to do. To do otherwise is to try to control the markets—something that is only reserved for God and natural disasters. Secondly, selling at the top and buying at the bottom does not guarantee profits. How many times have you heard of traders who managed to sell near the highs or buy near the bottoms, only to miss the ensuing move completely. Instead of making a full swing's profits, they managed to make only several ticks before they closed out their positions.

When you position comfortably into a profitable position, eliminate reasons that are not market-generated and might force you out of it. Find other sources to pay your rent, utility bills, or telephone bills. What you encounter in the real world must not be translated into what the markets are doing to your profitable positions. If you do, you won't be in the business for long if the markets turn choppy and more difficult to trade.

If you are long in the markets and are showing a profit, but you suddenly have an urge to get rid of your winners without any acceptable market-generated reason, execute only one type of trade as a stop-gap measure. Not selling out longs isn't an action, but a passive response. A positive action would be to execute a trade that will add to your position. This will satisfy your need for market action without giving up your winner.

Another way to force yourself to stick with winners is to look elsewhere to initiate plays. If you are long in one market that is acting well, try to find another market to play around in if you have the need for market action. Diversification of assets and equity inadvertently creates this escape valve response. Diversify and look at more market opportunities elsewhere to avoid tampering with your winners.

Once you have initiated a trade that starts to act like a winner, use stop orders to protect your profits and cut your losses. Protecting profits and cutting losses are two entirely different actions. Once your stop orders are correctly placed, you won't have any need to tamper with the position.

Making or losing money is a very emotional subject to deal with and we all bring a different set of parameters to trading because of this. Some of us use the markets to work out hostilities in our everyday lives, often with disastrous results. Treat trading as a business and you will learn to treat the wins and losses in the marketplace with more detachment.

The only way to make money in the market is to nurture winning positions. If you liquidate your winners, you will never have the opportunity to watch them make more money for you. The other strategy of getting rid of winners and using your capital to look for other winners is not a good one because every time you take on a new position you are taking on new market risks. If you have a winner, nurture it and it will grow into bigger profits.

Nurturing positions that will only break even is a waste of time and the time value of money. Losing positions definitely do not make money. Attention to losers is important because it protects your trading capital. No capital, no more trading.

RULE 32

Never Permit Speculative Ventures To Turn into Investments

This rule started as two separate rules, but the second rule, "Money lost by speculation is small compared to money lost in investments," contained many of the same points covered in this chapter. In fact, I have found that in the markets everything is so interrelated that it is very hard to make strong dichotomies of two ideas. Some aspect of any idea is related to another idea.

This is why it is so difficult to become a proficient trader in a short period of time. All trading ideas must be understood in totality at any one point in time, yet each fragmented idea can stand by itself. Complete mastery of individual principles of successful trading often gives you a false belief that you can trade successfully. In fact, you are only able to trade successfully under the limited market conditions then prevailing. If conditions change, as they often do to accommodate changing influences, you would be like a ship without a rudder—floating aimlessly.

There is often muddled thinking when you put on investments and speculations. The inability to define what type of trading you do will result in large losses and continued future bad trading habits. Are you a speculator or are you an investor?

Although so many concepts in the market are interrelated, you must be able to differentiate between investments and speculations. They differ in terms of objectives, time duration, and the amount of capital involved.

Speculation comes from the Latin word, *speculari*, which means "to observe." Speculation involves taking chances on ventures that could turn into profitable situations. You go into speculations knowing that you might lose all your capital. Investment involves using your capital for income or profit. Investments try to provide revenues, whereas in speculation the primary play is capital gains. Of the two, investments are of a longer duration.

Experienced traders never mix the two approaches. They have conditioned themselves to discriminate what type of approach to use in different market situations. Unsuccessful traders cannot discriminate differences in market situations. They will often trade long term with situations that can only provide quick speculator's profits or invest in speculative positions when market conditions do not warrant holding positions for longer than a day. Those who cannot define the current market, cannot manage the risks it will present. They will get embroiled in market situations over which they have no control and are sure to lose money.

Investments and speculations also differ in terms of time duration: short-term or long-term. As mentioned earlier, speculators are looking for quick profits without much regard for fundamental valuations. In fact, fundamentals are used only to isolate undervalued or overvalued market prices. Once the position is established, the trader seeks to equalize the temporary price and valuation disparity.

Investors, on the other hand, respect fundamentals. They regard minor price fluctuations as noise action revolving around a central valuation price that can increase or decrease. Instead of looking for instant market price revaluation due to temporary aberrations, investors look to have the fundamentals unfold over longer time periods.

This discussion of time duration and market analysis approaches brings to mind the age-old debate over which school of analysis is more appropriate—fundamental or technical.

The answer is that both are appropriate at different price levels of the markets. At low prices, fundamentals are more important in helping to determine whether or not to accumulate positions. (Please note that I say "accumulate" positions, not "liquidate.") At low prices, the profit to be made is limited by the fact that prices cannot get below zero. To be absurd, this is a stop loss order at a price of zero.

Technical analysis is more appropriate for high-priced issues or futures. Price action is so volatile at the upper end of prices that there must be more emphasis on liquidating long positions or, for the more speculative trader, on shorting particular markets. Once price moves away from high levels, they move violently away. Fundamentals may correctly account for bearish price action, but by the time correct fundamental analysis is made, price would have moved much too far away for the trader to capitalize on such information.

This type of phased-in market approach—fundamental or technical—has been the secret of success for money managers like John Templeton and Warren Buffet. If they are using fundamental analysis, these managers thrive when markets are moving from an accumulation stage to higher prices. Warren Buffet has even shut down his investment funds when he considered prices to have reached too high a level. With such overvaluation, he cannot find cheap stocks to buy, so he quits the game. John Templeton once thrived on fundamental analysis, but he has modified his approach by integrating arbitrage trading techniques into his investment paradigm. He invests in stocks of foreign countries and moved into currency arbitrage with exchange conversions.

Technical analysts thrive in violently active price action markets. This is why technical analysis is being applied so extensively to the stock market, where prices have quadrupled in the last six years. Technical analysis has always been used in the futures markets, which are subject to violent price actions. The leveraging factor in futures, where as little as 3 percent of the market valuation of the contract traded can be used to control the other 97 percent, is so great that the most minute relative price move can be reflected in drastic trading account equity drawdowns or increases.

Finally, there is the consideration of the amount of capital required to either speculate or invest. The speculator tries to put up as little money as possible, while the investor often puts up the full amount. People have the capital to speculate, but not invest, yet they go into situations as if they have the capital to invest. (For more ideas on this, see the discussion of scalpers, day traders, and long-term traders in Rule 27.)

How, then, do you learn to speculate when speculating is warranted and invest when investing is warranted? Aside from spending five years figuring out intuitively what market conditions warrant what trading approach, the only solution is to have two separate accounts—one for speculation, another for investments. This solution was presented to me by David Goldberg, a long-time member of the Chicago Board of Trade.

I had talked to David years ago about my inability to hang on to my winners and cut my losses short. I had been trading IBM stock and IBM options in the same trading account. After I sold out my IBM stock at slight profits I saw the stock go to new highs. The amount of money I left on the table was so great that I felt awful. Then, when I had IBM stock trades that were initial losers, I wouldn't get rid of them.

David suggested that I open two accounts—one for speculation and one for investments. He also told me that I should have bought IBM stock, which I wanted to hang on to for a long-term play in the investment account, and traded IBM stock from the speculation account for a short-term play. I thought it was foolish to have two accounts to trade just one stock because I was fixated on the redundant mechanics of creating two accounts. He, however, was making a very subtle point about the psychology and attitude a trader has towards a stock.

With two separate accounts, the long-term trade of IBM stock would have warranted a long-term outlook. If the stock dipped a quarter point from where I purchased it, I wouldn't panic. If it rallied a quarter point, I wouldn't be itching to take profits. If it dropped five points I wouldn't worry about it because it was a long-term trade. If it showed a five-point profit I still wouldn't unload, but would patiently wait for another five-point profit.

The speculation account would accommodate short-term trading strategies. If the same company's stock, IBM, was placed in the short-term account, I would panic if it dipped a quarter point and would try to unload it. If it rallied a quarter point, I would look to take profits immediately. I would never allow a five-point profit or loss to accumulate in the stock.

In this manner I would know exactly what is expected of me in managing each trading account. If the same stock was not doing what I designed the strategy to do in that account, I would liquidate that position. A side benefit is that I would not be able to rationalize my losses so easily, which is a problem with all unsuccessful traders.

There is no need to worry about profitable situations because you have defined each account, and each account performs to expectations. Getting profitable situations from each at the same time with the same stock is a god-send, but not in the game plan.

R U L E 3 3

Don't Try To Predetermine
Your Profits

When I was a customer's man years ago, I always was
asked one question to which I never knew the answer. If I
saw a profitable play in the market, I would tell my clients about it. After I disclosed the fundamental and technical reasons why a particular market should be bought
or sold, clients always asked how high or low I thought
the market would go. They wanted my projections.

Naively, I would make some half-hearted guesses of
where I expected the markets to go. Often, the market
would get there and go beyond those initial projections.
After having seen too many of these scenarios played out
I modified my off the cuff projections by adding the
phrase, " . . . at least," to my projections. Now, I won't even
bother with coming up with projected numbers. When
asked where the market is headed, I just say, "If it's a
bull market, you've got to be long; if it's a bear market,
you've got to be short."

I was caught off guard recently when Ben Larson, the host of Chicago's longest running television program on the stock markets, asked me to project the next day's market action. Trading for my own account over these many years has conditioned me to not talk about the markets to anyone, let alone his viewing audience. I blurted out, "Well, Ben, it looks like we might be up ten points tomorrow." Had I ended the interview with that statement, I would have looked brilliant because the market did go up 9.86 points the next day. Instead, I negated it by saying, "Maybe we will even be down ten points." A colleague who saw the interview later mentioned that I sounded like an idiot, and I agreed. In reality, I couldn't have cared less where the market was headed the next day. I was bullish and I was long. That was all that mattered to me.

Consider the market as composed of two types of actions: a meandering type of action where prices don't move much, and a trending type of action where prices move violently.

When you initiate a trade, you buy a market at a fixed price. Your analysis shows that the price you bought is a good price area. You are acting on the here and now, and you want the market to appreciate in value. When the market starts to go up you don't have any idea where it will stop. You might have a projection of some price top, but you don't really know. The only way you will know is when the price actually makes a top and starts to head down. As much as we try to use all our technical tools we really do not know what future events will be, especially price action.

Limited by our inability to forecast precisely what prices will be in the future, we do what we consider the next best thing: We initiate positions based on the premise that a trend in motion stays in motion. We know this premise is credible because of our own observations of price charts. Prices move up and they move down. However, we must not conclude that a trend in motion will stop at a future price that is arbitrarily determined with present tense information. This is a flaw of many unsuccessful traders who have initiated long positions. Once their price objectives are reached, they unload their positions, only to see the market continue past their selling points. *Again, there is absolutely no reason why prices will stop at the points you predetermine.*

If the price of whatever you are long has enough fundamental and technical reasons to move higher, eventually past your initial entry point, you must know that the conditions affecting that market have changed to accommodate new information (in most cases, information that you did not predict). If you cannot forecast in advance what this new information is, what makes you think that you can forecast some price objectives that the market has yet to reach? If you try to preordain where the market you are long will end, you will limit your potential profits.

For example, if you had gone long an S&P 500 index futures contract at 310 because it looked both fundamentally and technically bullish, you would have acted correctly on half the trade. The other half, that of allowing market action to cause the price of your holding to appreciate in value, must be played correctly. If you want to be a winning trader, you cannot send in limit orders to sell at some higher price before knowing the actual conditions affecting that market.

When you place an order to buy, you expect the price to move up after your purchase. Why else would you buy? (Strangely enough, there are those masochistic traders who buy fully expecting the markets to go down afterwards. Their problems go deeper than the solutions this book can provide.) In a similar manner, when you place an order to sell, you expect the price to move down after your sale. Again, why else would you sell? The fact that you have created an order to sell at a higher price in your mind when you go long means that you are not allowing the market to tell you what it wants to do. Instead, you are dictating to the market what you want it to do by telling it at what level you want it to stop moving up.

One of the best ways I know of to move with the flow of the market is to use stop loss orders that trail market action. In the case where you enter an order to sell at a predetermined level of profits, your action is active in the markets. In the case where you follow the market up with trailing stop sell orders to protect your profits, your action is passive. When you are passive, you allow the market to tell you when it wants you to get out.

RULE 34

Never Buy a Stock Because It Has a Big Decline from Its Previous High, nor Sell a Stock Because It Is High Priced

In assessing market conditions to determine your trading strategy, it is always better to buy at cheaper prices than higher prices. As a general rule, it is best to try to find bargain stocks as defined by low prices. However, there are times when buying at a lower prices is not warranted.

Market action and where the price of an issue or futures has come from is a good indication of whether or not you should buy it after a decline from a previous high or sell it because it is high priced. It is more important to find out where you are in the market cycle.

One of the cleverest methods of distributing stocks or futures has been to get prospective buyers to believe that they are buying something at bargain prices. We have been conditioned by stores or anybody wanting to unload products to expect lowered prices when sales are offered. The same approach is used to unload stocks or futures to potential buyers. The products that the market offers are different in concept, utility, and function from store-bought items, yet the appeals to buy are the same.

In the case of a "retracement," you must use previous market action to help you determine whether it is a reaction in a bull market or a reversal from a bull market to a bear market. How you assess the current situation determines how you trade the markets. If the market is still bullish despite a reaction, you can continue to buy the dips. On the other hand, if the market has abruptly changed from bullish to bearish in one sell-off, continued buying into the weakness will turn into buying into a bear market. The former situation is a harbinger of profits to come and the latter is an omen of losses.

In assessing the current market's condition, you must be able to compare the current situation with past behavior. If the market has hit an all-time high and backs off, you must determine if the retracement is normal for this market. One way to determine this is to see what the past reactions were like. Since you can gauge market action according to three types of technical data—price, time, and volume—you can compare current price, time, or volume action with the most recent action. You want to determine how similar the current actions are relative to the most recent action. The most recent action must have been a normal reaction in a bull market, otherwise you would not have had a continued move into new price high territory. If the current action, with time, price, or volume viewpoints, differs remarkably from the most recent action, then perhaps a trend reversal is imminent: The bull market has ended and a bear market will ensue.

If a market has been going into new highs for several weeks and reacts for the first time, you must observe this reaction, not for what it is doing now, but to compare it with future reactions. If it drops back by 10 percent in price, note the sell-off. When it resumes its upward move and encounters a second sell-off, watch to see if it reacts less than 10 percent or more than 10 percent. If it reacts less than previously, or less than 10 percent, the market is probably reacting normally. If, on the other hand, it reacts more than 10 percent, then you know something is not right with this bullish move. It is possible that the market has seen its top.

Since the markets are defined according to three parameters, it is critical that you not only observe price reactions, but also length of time that the reactions take to transpire. If the reaction lasted seven trading days and the second reaction reacts for more than seven days before the market goes back up, then you know that something again is not right. Volume analysis is critical also, except that the analysis of volume disparities is not as precise and requires more subjective judgment.

As you can see, successful trading is based on observations of market actions. However, indiscriminately observing price, time, or volume action is not beneficial. At a very basic level you must observe and then compare. Your comparison of two activities must produce definite differences. You can then go on to other analytical techniques to confirm or disprove your observations.

Hence, it is important for you to see what the current reaction is like when compared to the previous reactions. Just because the market has had a reaction after punching through new highs on the upside does not mean that you continue to go buy on any dip. You must determine if the last high was the very last high.

In the same manner, you must observe that not all new highs can be sold. As a scalper you can get away with selling new highs most of the time, but as a day trader or a longer-term trader, the new highs must be viewed with respect. The market that has the strength to punch through new highs is doing two things: checking for stop buy orders on the upside and showing massive strength.

Floor traders and scalpers like to test where the stop orders are, be they on the sell or buy side. Stop orders rest above or below the current market range. If the market has enough strength to make relative highs, it has enough strength to continue in that direction. Stop orders are instituted by traders to limit market losses. If the scalpers can offer the market up by constantly offering supply at higher and higher prices, eventually the stop buy orders will be touched. Once touched, they can be executed either at the market or at a limit price. The scalpers can sell into this short covering buying by traders. However, the fact that there is enough strength to push prices to these relatively higher prices implies that there is very good buying going on.

If the markets are strong enough to make new highs, they will continue to make new highs. Despite the fact that the last high is always the all-time high, in order to get to this last high the market had to make progressively higher and higher prices. This is strength. You don't want to sell the higher highs hoping that the last high you sold will be the all-time high. The odds are not in your favor to make money: For the one time that you do sell the high, you would have to cover your shorts immediately after selling all those other intermediate highs. Play with the odds in your favor.

Instead of selling new highs, look to buy new highs and have enough capital to sustain the intermediate retracements after the highs are made. (See Rule 28 on Harold Goodman and his buying into new highs for a more detailed explanation of this rule.)

RULE 35

Become a Buyer As Soon As a Stock Makes New Highs After a Normal Reaction

This rule is similar to the rules about not selling new highs and making sure that the reaction following a new high is not the last reaction. However, the rule in this chapter is a positive statement with action. It tells you how to make a profitable position trade. The other rules, which tell you how to prevent losses, are passive.

When a market trades away from a range to the upside, it is showing its strength. Once it moves out of the trading range you can expect one of two actions: Either the market will run violently to the upside, or it will fake you out by backtracking to the lower end of the trading range. What clues does the market offer to help you determine which way it is headed?

In the case where the market runs violently to the upside, you will see quite a few market participants getting on board for the up move. These include both scalpers turned day traders, who are buying into new highs or covering shorts sold at lower prices, and long-term traders who are adding to their positions. The long-term traders are the ones who fuel the up move. Scalpers and day traders do not have enough buying strength to cause a sustained move in the market. Once the shorter-term traders have a quick profit with the position they have on, they are likely to release that position into the market to take profits. On the other hand, long-term traders will buy on a breakout to the upside and keep their holdings out of the floating supply. This helps to sustain the upward momentum.

Once the market makes a sustained upward move, this rule stipulates that if it backs off and then takes out the previous high it is profitable to buy further breakouts. Visually, this is seeing a previous top broken to the upside. Inspecting this from the perspective of conventional chart pattern analysis, what you are seeing is the breakout of a single top.

There are upside breakouts of two and sometimes three previous high levels established at around the same price levels. With the increasing numbers of similar high price level tops, there is greater strength in the ensuing upside breakout: A breakout of a triple top is stronger than a double top breakout, and a double top breakout is stronger than a single top breakout.

Even within the breakouts to the upside of single, double, or triple tops, there is always the possibility, not the probability, that the breakouts could be false. Conventional chart analysis stipulates that if the market does not pursue an upward move after a breakout, then it is considered a false breakout. This is not quite the case. It is considered a false breakout if there is no follow-through on the upside *and* if prices fall back to previous low levels and remain there. This is a real false breakout.

If the market breaks above the previous tops and backs off, it can regain and amass more strength as it waits for another assault on the previous highs. It is important here to observe and record the price level that stops the sell-off of this false breakout. When the market reaches for new highs, it must stay above the previous lows in order to show strength. This previous sell-off low is now the benchmark of strength. If the previous lows do not hold after the market takes out the most recent high, then it can be considered a false breakout.

Volume is a consideration here because price action that takes out previous highs serves only to warn traders that some important resistance levels are possibly being challenged. Price action under these conditions does not forecast whether or not the breakout will be sustained. Price action at much higher levels will only confirm the strength that is evident.

If the market backs away from a new high, it is normal for the volume of activity to remain the same or to become somewhat lighter. This reflects a declining interest in selling the market when prices go lower. It does not mean that there will be increasing interest in selling at higher prices as shown by increasing volume activity, although that is to be expected. Whatever the reasons for light volume on normal downside action, the successful trader will observe volume both on normal reactions and on successive challenges to previous highs. If the trader can observe light volume on sell-offs and increasing volume on new high price challenges, he or she will correctly analyze the current market condition as being valid upside breakouts.

RULE 36

The Human Side of Every Person Is the Greatest Enemy to Successful Trading

Market professionals have always said that the inability to control the human element is the folly of the best traders. Throughout history we have seen the great speculators like Jesse Livermore and Arthur Cutten fall by the wayside when their trading approaches were misapplied to changing market conditions. Recently great speculators like Richard Dennis have failed when they applied once-applicable trading approaches to new market conditions.

It is an axiom in market folklore that the market will do whatever it has to do, to do the most damage to the most people. And the markets are situated extremely well to do this.

We humans, however, are frail. We can eat in only one way—through our mouths. We see in only one manner—when we open our eyes. We can feel and smell in only limited ways—when we touch with our skin and inhale through our noses. Yet we persist, foolishly at times, in regarding the markets to be as frail and as singular as we are. Some of us think that the markets are always in a trading range, so we always use trading market analytical techniques. Others contend that markets are always trending and therefore use trending market techniques all the time. Still others believe that markets are purely random and no single analytical approach is useful. The folly of humans is that some of us continue to use tools that are no longer applicable with new conditions. We assume that, once the markets are in any particular stage of activity, they will remain in that state.

There are times when successful trading or investing demand that a particular trading technique be used. There are other times when no *one* technique will work. Work on your personality to be flexible enough to change when change is warranted.

There is a time for everything, even in the markets. If there is inflexibility on the part of the trader there is failure.

Compounding the problems confronting inflexible traders is another problem inherent in the trading profession itself—stress. A Gallup poll conducted for the *Wall Street Journal* in August 1987 (reported in the September 29, 1987, edition), found that the job with the highest stress rating was commodity trading. Seventy-four percent of executives surveyed stated that trading involved the most stress, followed by advertising (42 percent), investment banking (21 percent), high technology (15 percent), legal profession (7 percent) and insurance (6 percent).

To alleviate this stress, traders often try the wrong solutions: they drink, they smoke, they do drugs. The successful trader deals with stress by picking and choosing the markets and conditions that he or she will trade in, virtually guaranteeing success.

But most people won't deal with trading stress in this manner because they have ingrained reasons to justify their successes elsewhere. To win in their own business, they must lose at trading. To feel good about making money quick and fast in the markets, they must work harder at their jobs. This is the wrong conditioning to the right responses.

As humans, we find varied ways to sabotage our successes in the markets. Some find the markets to be a very efficient way to sublimate seething emotions. If a trader argues at home, he won't let a trade get the best of him. He'll lose his shirt rather than have a market loser force him to do something he doesn't want to do. There's no way the trade is going to get the best of him, especially after his wife was so wrong.

As humans, we are not sure of ourselves. We rely on the experts in the trading business to guide us. Some of us even want experts to take over the management. Brokers are asked to do more trading for clients because the client is too busy to manage the money. These are the wrong reasons to trade. *You must trade because you want to make money.*

If you are unsuccessful at trading, stop for a moment and think about the real reasons you want to trade. Do you want to escape a boring job? Do you want to impress your friends? Such reasons are not strong enough to sustain traders while they learn the difficult business of trading. Make sure that you are trading to make money, and not because you want escapes.

Lack of confidence is a detriment to successful trading. Most unsuccessful traders don't have the nerves to pull the trigger. They take reckless shots in the markets and lose money. This, instead of abetting their confidence, reinforces their lack of it. If they were so good, why did they lose money?

You cannot do anything about the past; yet you can recognize the problems that being human pose for you as a successful trader. If you run into a string of losses, stop trading for a while. Take a break and come back again with all those problems resolved or held in abeyance.

RULE 37

Ban Wishful Thinking in the Markets

The market acts on logic—its own logic. To be a successful trader, you must think like the market thinks and act like the market acts. This is the beginning of a regimen of appropriate actions that includes money, capital risk, and position management. Unsuccessful traders are those who feel that the markets must think and act like the traders do. Wishful thinking is one of many unsuccessful trading habits.

The enigma of market action is that at one stroke it encompasses reality, where market losses are immediate and brutal, and fantasy, where prices can be driven up or down beyond all expectations. Wishful thinking, uncoupled with a healthy perception of reality, is the application of fantasy to market actions.

Vic Rydberg was a trader at one of Chicago's futures exchanges and a very capable money manager. Before becoming a trader, he had been a professional thoroughbred handicapper. After graduating from college in the 1930s, he worked one year as an engineer. He found handicapping horses more interesting and embarked on a successful career playing the ponies "all the way from Florida to California." The ability that he developed to manage his risk capital while betting on horses made him an extremely successful handicapper. Unfortunately, this ability precluded him from being successful as a futures trader.

In retrospect I can see that because he was so successful in position management when he bet on the ponies he failed to learn the other important aspects of the markets when he tried to trade successfully. His risk management skills allowed Vic to stay in the trading game. He was successful in the sense that he survived, but unsuccessful in the sense that he made no real money. He was halfway to becoming a very successful trader.

This chapter is not about his success in risk management and his ability to stay in a game which he hardly knew anything about, but about the ramifications of his ability to manage risk successfully. He was very prone to wishful thinking. He had a tendency to rationalize market actions that did not unfold according to his scenarios, and his trading profits suffered as a consequence of this.

Vic showed a disregard for market realities one day in his corn positions. The floor had expected an extremely bullish supply report for the existing corn crop. Vic had positioned well ahead of the report and bought a few contracts. He had no idea where he should liquidate his position if the market reacted badly to the bullish reports. All professionals must have an idea of where they get out if they are wrong.

The report came in extremely bullish, far more than anybody on the floor had expected. The market had closed for the day, so the next morning's expectations were that corn would open much higher, wheat higher, and soybeans higher to unchanged. Wheat opened higher and soybeans opened higher to unchanged, both according to floor traders' expectations. Corn, however, opened unchanged. It did not open lower, which would have been extremely bullish, and it did not open higher, which would have been according to expectations.

Most market players act more on fears and expectations than they do on reality. Had corn opened up, market action would have confirmed their expectations and they would have continued to move the prices up by buying more for themselves or getting others to buy. Because corn opened unchanged and failed to go up from the opening, the players had their worst fears confirmed.

As it turns out, corn prices dropped severely and touched limit down. They bounced up off limit, and then they traded down again. First the May option touched limit. Then the July option touched limit. Then September, then December. Finally, all one could see from the quote boards on the walls of the exchange was that everything was down the limit for the day. Then a pool of sell orders started to come in. First, it was 5,000 contracts offered limit down on the May option. Then a few hundred were offered in the new crop, December. By the end of the day, several million bushels of corn were offered in July, the end of the old crop. All across the board, millions of bushels of corn were offered for sale at limit down prices.

As soon as prices in the new crop corn overcame the sell orders by rallying from limit down, the sell orders cascaded into the front months. As corn prices remained limit down, the selling started to go into the wheat pit. First, they knocked the prices off the high for wheat. On the opening, wheat had rallied to intraday highs. Traders who were long corn had to sell something to hedge their losing positions outside of the corn pit because nobody wanted to buy corn. Some picked wheat to sell. Others picked oats. Still others picked soybeans.

Vic was in the pit that morning with the rest of the traders trying to make sense of the market action. His perception of the market was turning into wishful thinking. I observed several stages in this process as the day wore on.

The first stage was denial of market action. Vic had expected the market to go up after the report. He had not planned on exiting his trades, except with profits, so he held onto his positions. Prices, however, continued to erode.

The second stage was the reinforcement of his initial decision to buy because it's bullish. Vic and other traders crowded around the Reuters broadtape machine to check the government reports. They all concurred that the reports were bullish and that being long was the right thing to do. Even in the late afternoon, they were hopeful that buying would come in and show them they were right. They consulted other demand reports and began reading between the lines: Russia would buy because it still had to fulfill a portion of its commitment for the year; China would buy because it was facing a severe drought; and India would buy because the monsoons had flooded the croplands. Prices, however, fell further.

The third stage crept in slowly. At this point they thought wishfully, hoped against reality, prayed for the miracle. As the market, several cents away from limit down, lulled observers to sleep and agitated long-sided traders, the fear that possibly no buy orders would come in germinated in one section of the trading pit. Before long, it became pervasive. One by one, the traders yawned in the pit, looked at their trading cards, and tallied their longs. They turned around and held their hands outwards. One offered 50 corn contracts, another offered 10. As traders started to unload, prices gave way and the market slid down like a hot knife through butter. Vic was able to unload his position on the next day's opening, which was several cents from limit down.

Vic buttonholed me shortly afterwards to talk about what had happened. All his sentences began with "It's bullish because . . ." and ended with ". . . I can't figure it out."

Wishful thinking now preempted rational thought.

Markets don't behave as you wish, but as they please. Markets have their own logic, and you must be able to discern what they are trying to tell you. The first consideration is: Is your trading equity appreciating or eroding? If the market does not conform to your game plan, you cannot stay with a position that is eroding your equity. That's wishful thinking. The equity you are losing is the market's way of telling you that, for whatever reasons, your market analysis was wrong. Take your loss and figure it out later.

RULE 38

Big Movements Take Time To Develop

In another chapter I talk about how important it is to use patience if you want to make substantial profits in the markets. The onset of options trading has caused some traders to move away from this philosophy of successful trading.

Trading history was made in 1973, when the Chicago Board Options Exchange, an offshoot of the Chicago Board of Trade, began trading listed stock options with standardized contracts. Until then, there were only two ways to make money in the stock markets: playing the right side of long-term trends to make capital gains and making above-average returns on dividends. The futures markets only have capital gains play. (However, in a sophisticated play with cost-of-carry markets, spreaders can make money on interest rates by buying the front end and selling the back end of an intramarket spread. The spreader takes delivery of the front end and holds it to deliver on the short side of the spread when it is due. The difference between the actual cost of carrying the futures contract and the delivered price of the short side of the spread is the profit. This play is difficult for the small speculator to implement because the margins of profits are razor thin.) All markets have capital gains plays, but only the capital markets have the interest coupons or dividends returns, the cost-of-carry play.

Before options came on the investment scene, there were no profitable ways to make money in markets that were trendless or had no sustained trending moves. When trends did occur, they unfolded over several years in the case of stocks and bonds, and several months in the case of futures. Options could be used to make money in *all* markets. In violently upward markets, speculators could make money by buying calls or selling puts. In down markets, puts could be bought or calls could be sold. In trendless markets, both calls and puts could be sold. In this manner, the speculator could now make money in sideways markets.

For the first time in market history, speculators could efficiently make money in markets that did not move. Sideways movements more often lead to up markets than to down markets. The traditional speculators waited for the up moves to begin so that they could latch onto the potential capital gains. Sideways markets did not move enough so that speculators could make any profits. However, they could make money with options by watching the markets erode the call and put premiums.

With the advent of options and the high profile of the trading range markets, the trader's skills in analyzing when a bull market or a bear market began or ended were no longer needed to make money on capital gains plays. Now, inexperienced younger traders who had no concept of how a bull or a bear market behaved could just sell put and call premiums. As the options eroded, the young traders' trading equity increased. For once, there was no need for new traders to accumulate market experience. As an options trader, all you had to do was to arbitrage differences in prices and sell premiums.

Options changed the behavior of the underlying market. The action of the stock market, where equity options took hold the earliest, illustrates the point I'm trying to make. The years from the beginning of 1986 to the end of 1988 saw three distinct market moves.

The first move saw the Dow Jones industrial averages climb from around the 1,900 level to the 2,700 level in less than one year. This historic surge was partially fueled by the options traders.

Then followed the quickest drop in history: The industrial averages lost one-third of their valuation in a two-month period, again fueled by options traders who called their strategy "portfolio insurance." The fact that the options players got bloodied the most in this market underscores the fact that the excesses caused by the use of options had to be compensated for by the violence of a one-day, 508-point drop. The outright short sellers—not the options players—made a bundle of money.

The stock market then staged one of the longest trading range markets after the sharpest drop. Again this was of historical significance, and again the premium sellers were actively making money. Markets such as these would not have existed before the options markets took hold. In making it easier for new traders to make money in the markets by selling premiums, we lost the need for analyzing market conditions.

The cycle has made one complete revolution and we are now back at the beginning of all market strategies: Determine the trend of the market to make the most money. The young traders who have made big money in options will be forced to fall back on traditional ways of analyzing market movements if they want to take advantage of capital gains plays.

There is no free lunch in this business. Successful traders make money in long, drawn out bull markets. These are markets that take time to develop.

RULE 39

Don't Be Too Curious About Reasons Behind the Moves

As a college student majoring in psychology, one of the least enjoyable courses I ever took was one on learning theory, taught by a stuffy professor of cognitive learning who eventually became the chairman of the department. We studied nonsense syllables for one quarter. Nonsense syllables are created by three or more randomly selected letters of the alphabet. The instructors asked us to memorize them for later recall. Twenty years later, I now know what they were trying to teach us: the pain and agony of wasting time learning nonsense.

One day, while wondering about the real-world application of memorizing nonsense syllables, I got up and walked out of the class. The professor later called me aside and asked me what the problem was. I told him that I couldn't see the reason for memorizing meaningless strings of letters. Another day I stood up in class and tried to explain what I thought was going on with the lists of syllables we were trying to learn. The professor cleared his throat and answered, "It really doesn't matter what you think. You're in this class for predetermined reasons. My role is to instruct you in what has been observed in the past. You think on your own, but you can't affect this class."

The markets are often like the nonsense syllables in my cognitive learning class: They act the way they do for whatever reasons they do. Knowing the reasons behind current market behavior is a bonus to successful market trading, but it is not a prerequisite.

The human mind, however, must have reasons why one action occurred and another didn't. The human mind is a mass of interlocking cells, while memory is the connection of these cells into particular patterns that can be traversed again in the future. Successful trading does not require traversing patterns again in the brain, but does require knowing when to take profits and cut losses. If a futures contract unexpectedly makes a new high, the mind immediately seeks an explanation. Deciding whether to add a position in the direction of the new high or to establish a level to take profits is not enough. In order to pigeonhole the price action and recall it later as an experience, the mind must tie the action to other dendrites and synapses existent in the brain.

To the extent that you can retrieve explanations that reinforce the market's underlying bullish or bearish trend, you can correctly trade the markets for profits. But problems appear when you retrieve information that goes counter to the trend and then attempt to pick tops or bottoms. You may or may not be successful. This depends on whether the market has integrated the information you retrieved, which would call for a reversal in price trends. If the markets have not integrated this revolutionary piece of information, you may find yourself shorting at the top to only cover at higher prices or buying at the bottom only to sell at lower prices.

Extending this problem, what exact piece of information can one retrieve that would have a direct impact on market prices, the ultimate gauge of market success? Richard Dennis once said that prices are the markers by which he was considered successful. Studying and analyzing anything else would be begging the question of how to trade successfully.

When there are price movements, either in your favor or against your position, you must initially determine whether you can take profits or do something to limit your losses. If you choose to wait "while Rome burns," you are preventing yourself from becoming a successful trader by being an unsuccessful analyst. When the reason is known, it will be too late for you to act on it.

If you think that your analysis might eventually be correct even though the price action is not reflecting it, don't be afraid that you will miss the moves. If the price action is confirmed by trend-supporting information, you can always get on board after missing only slight profits. For this increased assurance, you have given up only a few ticks or points. If information does not confirm the price action, you wouldn't have been able to capitalize on your supposedly "correct information" because the market price never proved you right.

R U L E   4 0

Look for Reasonable Profits

We've all heard stories about people making a lot of money in the markets. Perhaps you know someone who bought Time stock just before the buyout, in which it shot up $47 in one day, or someone who bought soybeans just before the drought. The beans moved from $5.50 a bushel to more than $10 a bushel. That's about a $21,000 move on one contract in two months. These events don't occur often, but when these events do occur and are reported in the media, the public is led to believe that making 100 percent a year or more on one's capital is the norm.

I have made an average 50 percent net return on my own investments and speculations without opening margin and haircut accounts. This includes all the years in which I broke even or lost money in the markets because I was learning about the business and all the years in which I broke even or lost money in the markets because I was an expert.

I started trading with about $5,000 in my account. During the first year I scalped like crazy and made about a $30,000 profit at the end of the year. I made about a 600 percent return on my original capital. Of course, being young and inexperienced, I spent all of my profits. At the start of the second year, I wondered how much return I could get for the amount of capital I was using. Would it be 600 percent again, or could I double it to maybe 1,200 percent? At the end of the second year I again turned my $5,000 start capital to $30,000 of profits. Again I worked like a madman on the floor. And not knowing that even rainbows end somewhere I spent like a madman. At the start of the third year I had $5,000 in the account and wondered whether this would be the year in which I would double my profits. Of course, the question that I should have asked was how was I able to get two 600 percent return years in a row! As it evolved, the third year turned into a disaster.

Out of this experience I developed my own little rule of business management: I figured out that the harder I worked my money, the faster it went about finding other owners.

I know that if you spend time to learn about the markets and then trade and invest in them, you must get a better than average rate of return. The average rate of return is what the professionals pay you after they make their profits and overhead! This pays for your professional involvement in the markets.

However, once in a while there are stellar moves in the marketplace that will make a pauper a prince.

Professionals, because they are full-time players in the markets, have opportunities to latch onto such stellar moves once in a while. What most people don't understand is that in order to take advantage of such moves, they must have enough capital in their accounts to handle larger than normal positions. They must also have resources to research their investments or speculations and support people on the floor to handle the execution of their trades. In other words, they must have an infrastructure of support that will allow them to capitalize on these plays. Most traders don't. They cannot jump from trading 10 contracts or 1,000 shares of stock to 100 contracts or 10,000 shares overnight.

Since most traders don't have the infrastructure already in place, they cannot take full advantage of the moves without risking their livelihood. If they can make better than average returns without stepping out of their normal trading environment, they will survive to capitalize on the next stellar move. And let me assure you that if you miss this one move, others will soon come along.

A colleague told me about an equity options trader who made $128,000 on $58,000 of trading capital in four months. This was about a 220 percent return on his capital, nonannualized. In the height of public participation in the options markets, profits were much higher because the markets were younger and less efficient.

What is not known about performances such as these is the actual net return. Under more discrete questioning I discovered that because of the margining of his positions, this trader was borrowing about $490,000 to cover his positions. His haircut was about $575,000. Through the magic of exchange and industry regulations, the trader increased his trading power by tenfold.

Then the expenses started to erode his profits. First there was the $5,000 a month overhead he had to pay to get computer equipment, data services, and clerical help. The trader paid himself no salary and worked strictly for profits. Then there were commission costs. As an exchange member, his commissions were as low as 30 cents a contract, yet they still amounted to $15,000 a month. His total overhead was about $20,000 a month.

For four months of activity, his total expenses amounted to about $80,000. Deducting this from his profits of $128,000, he netted about a $48,000 return every trimester. His annualized net profits would be about three times the $48,000, or $144,000. His weekly net profits were about $3,000. If he were to make $144,000 net profit every year and his commission costs amounted to $15,000 a month at 30 cents a contract (that comes out to 50,000 contracts traded every month), he would be making about 24 cents profit on each trade.

In a week of frenzied stock takeover activity, this trader lost $15,000. He had to close out his options positions in takeover stocks at big losses. One week of losses offset five weeks of profits.

Still, if you look at the amount of net profits at the end of the year, $144,000, and see what capital he had to do this with, $58,000, you would see that he was still making about a 248 percent net return a year. To get this return he had to take advantage of exchange membership and extremely beneficial margining and haircut regulations. If he had to come up with the full amount of haircut money, $575,000, to make $144,000 a year, his annual rate of return would fall to 25 percent a year.

A 25 percent annual rate of return is sustainable. A 248 percent rate of return is not sustainable on a long-term basis. The fact that the trader has beneficial capital requirements is balanced by the fact he is subject to volatile losses when the leveraging worked against him. Since he is a professional, he must know how to control his losses so that he can capitalize on his advantages.

If you want to trade the markets and make profits over the long term, you must not expect to sustain extremely high rates of return. In fact, you must be leery of situations that offer high rates over a short period, for they also carry an above-average risk of losing all your trading capital.

RULE 41

If You Can't Make Money Trading the Leading Issues, You Aren't Going To Make It Trading the Overall Markets

The original intent of this rule was to show that the leading issues led the rest of the markets. If you were not able to read the tape activity of the leading issues, and hence forecast their future movements, you would not be able to read what the rest of the market was doing.

The market moves in waves of buying and selling activity. The rule discussed in this chapter was conceived when the overall markets were traded as individual issues. As long as market players were only able to trade individual issues, if they had an opinion about the whole market the genie was contained in the bottle. Once the exchanges opened trading in indices and at margins that were even less than individual stock margins prior to the 1929 crash, a completely different set of market interpretations had to be created.

To understand how the market operates in waves of buying and selling activities, it is necessary to see how its various components interact with one another.

The stock market can be broken into three basic tiers or activity groups: the primary, the secondary, and the tertiary. These groups can be divided according to institutional interest, trading volume, and investment grades. For a quick and easy way of segregating these stocks into viable groups for analysis, just look at their prices. The primaries are the highest priced, the secondaries are the second highest, and the tertiary are the cheapest to own.

In the primary group we can see IBM, Digital Equipment, Procter & Gamble, General Motors, Ford Motors, Time, Inc., and other companies that are the backbone of the United States economy. They are the blue chips.

The secondary group comprises companies like Warner Communications, Paramount, USX Corporation, Syntex, Exxon, General Electric, American Express, and Motorola. The quality of these stocks is high and, depending on the fundamentals of these companies, they are sometimes found in the primary group. Texaco was once considered a blue-chip issue but is now classified as a secondary stock.

The tertiary group is made up of stocks that range from dogs to fallen blue chips like Navistar (formerly known as International Harvester) and Mansville (formerly known as Johns Mansville).

This categorization of the stock market is critical to being able to read market activity correctly. Overall market activity can be seen as buying and selling interests by market participants. Their overall buying and selling will be revealed in the strength and weakness of the three groups.

The bottom of a bear market is distinguished from the beginning of a bull market by activity in the primary groups of stocks. After all three groups of stocks have found bottoms at the end of a bear market, buying interests will first appear in the primary group. The big players like insurance companies, mutual funds, and heavily capitalized individuals will start to nibble at the fallen blue chips. Stocks that once traded at $100 and now are trading at $30 or $40 will be bought quietly. Technical indicators will show accumulation of these blue chips.

After a severe bear market, the uninformed investor will have no capital to accumulate stocks for long-term investments. Meanwhile, because the blue chips are the strongest companies financially, they can weather bear market fundamentals that have permeated the whole economy. The weaker companies have gone bankrupt, leaving the blue chips, by default, thriving on reduced market shares. The informed investors and companies know that the blue chips will survive.

In the process of buying the blue chips, the big players start to move up the prices. Supply decreases while demand increases. As prices of the blue chips move from the $30 to $40 range to the $60 to $70 range, the economy starts to improve. While this is happening, companies start to rehire the employees that they laid off during the bear market. As the workers replenish their investment coffers with money, they start to look at investable securities. The primaries have gone to recent highs and have moved out of the purchasing range of these recently enriched workers. The interest is now to look for value in secondary issues.

As the buying action moves to the secondaries, they climb from the $20 to $30 range to the $40 to $50 range. Meanwhile, the primaries continue to show strength either because of rotation activity, where prices are locked in a trading range, or because certain primary issues manage to double and quadruple in price due to particular situations that reflect heightened interest in whatever game Wall Street is playing at the time: In the 1960s it was conglomerates; in the 1980s it is mergers and acquisitions.

The moneyed investors rotate their interests in the primaries and create opportunities that will help them unload their much-appreciated holdings to other buyers.

Under the strength of leading issues they will unload the weaker sisters. Under the strength of IBM, other computer stocks like Texas Instruments and Digital Equipment will find more buyers.

As the primaries are rotated and the secondaries are accumulated and marked up, poorly capitalized investors start to wend their way into investment traps by looking at the tertiaries. Industry insiders have always regarded interests in the tertiary issues as a harbinger that the bull market is about over. As some market players look to value tertiary issues considerably above what fundamentals would justify, informed investors might even start to put out shorts in the secondary groups. The primary issues were the first to go up and they will be the last to go down.

As the unloading of the appreciated holdings continues, pockets of weakness appear in the leading issues. Once in a while a primary issue might drop several points for no apparent reason, while the rest of the market continues unchanged. This is one of the first signs that distribution is about over and a campaign to drive stocks down is about to begin.

Bear markets in stocks begin while the economy is still in a bull market. Under cover of darkness the enemy creeps in. The cycle then resumes. Bear markets cannot begin until informed investors have had a chance to unload their holdings. The collapse of the stock market in October 1987 was so fast that insiders were not able to unload their holdings. Since the bulk of the holders of the stocks at 2,750 on the Dow Jones industrials were also the holders of these stocks with the averages at 1,650, it was easier for them to buy more stock than to sell what they already owned.

The most popular technical analysis technique within the last 50 years has been the revival of the Elliott Wave theory developed by Ralph Nelson Elliott and popularized by Robert Prechter under the initial instructions of A. J. Frost. The Elliott Wave theory was originally conceived as a way to discern wave formations in the Dow Jones industrial averages. The patterns that unfolded could be used to interpret overall market activity. Some individual traders and analysts have been able to use the theory to discern similar patterns in individual stock issues and futures contracts.

Since the overall market could be forecasted with relative success, it was initially easy for wave followers to trade individual stock issues well. However, as early as 1984 I noticed that the Dow Jones industrials waves that formed from 1975 on did not follow previous formation creations. The corrections were becoming lengthier, and the impulse waves were becoming more violent.

The increasing polarity of violent impulse waves from lengthier corrective waves was accelerated by the fact that in 1984 Robert Prechter traded stock index options using the Elliott Wave theory with great success. His accomplishment was hailed throughout the investment world. There had been some interest in trading the indices with the Elliott Wave theory, but it was Prechter's phenomenal trading of index options that brought this trading approach into the light.

For once we witnessed a phenomenon the investment world had never seen before: Market interests that had been forced in the past to be played out in individual stock issues could now be played out in actual trading in the indices. Not only could it be played out in such a manner, it also could be traded with great success with a technique that worked very well: the application of the Elliott Wave theory.

As in all market trading strategies that eventually die because of their own successes, the same advantage that Elliott Wave theorists had over others when trading the Dow Jones industrial averages invalidated the Elliott

Wave theory. As long as others could not trade the indices using the Elliott Wave theory, it remained valid in forecasting wave movements. Once the indices could be traded using the theory, it no longer worked.

RULE 42

Leaders of Today May Not Be the Leaders of Tomorrow

There are many ways to forecast future price movements, but the most basic way is to look at past price action and try to determine a pattern. If you can see a pattern that repeats with a greater than 50 percent probability, you will be able to forecast future price movements. This does not necessarily mean that you will make money, for that is a question of position management.

In looking for stocks that lead the rest of the market, you are basically looking for a pattern that repeats. The money is not made by trading the leading stock, but by trading the stocks that follow it.

When the leader starts its move, traders start to buy stocks that have followed this leader in the past. The trader makes money when the followers eventually go up in price. Within the group of followers there are clearly defined degrees of how fast and how often they follow the leader. Knowing which of the follower stocks are laggards is also important because when the laggards no longer follow the follower stocks, the strength of the leader stock is diminishing. It is time to cut back the commitment of capital to the followers.

The leader can be an individual stock or a group of stocks in the same industry. In the intermediate bull market of 1986, the leader was a group of technology stocks that included IBM, Texas Instruments, Digital Equipment and Hewlett Packard. These technology stocks were led by IBM. Once IBM found its intermediate target, it rotated nicely in a trading range while the other technology stocks followed it up. As soon as traders saw IBM move, they started picking up on the nontechnology stocks, and eventually the whole market went up.

There is one problem with following the leader stock over time: The strength of the stock eventually flags, and other stocks take over as the leaders. One way to discern when the mantle of strength is being handed over to other issues is by observing how the laggard stocks behave. In normal markets, where the follower stocks move up after the lead stock makes new highs for the move, the laggard stocks also will follow to the upside in their own proportionate pricing. If the leader moves five points in a week, the laggards might only move two points. If the laggards retreat instead of move, the strength of the overall market is in question.

Another way to observe the weakness of the leader stock is to watch stocks that in the immediate past followed the leader upwards. If the leader stock stops going up, watch what the immediate followers are doing. If immediate followers show strength and continue upwards, you can conclude that market strength is being transferred to the followers. The current leader will soon become a follower.

Follower stocks also have rotational strength. The Digital Equipments and the Hewlett Packards of their respective industries will take over the lead when the leader falters. Because of the number of issues available in the markets today, it is best to define market strength by industry. Barron's and Standard & Poor's have created their own industry groups. By creating composite numbers for each industry group, traders can monitor the activity of one group relative to other groups.

The analysis of relative price movements can be used also with futures contracts—within futures contracts themselves (soybeans) and within a futures complex such as grains or metals.

In the first case, within futures contracts themselves, you can observe strengths or weaknesses among different expiration months in the same contract. For example, you can track and compare the relative price movements of each of the expiration months. This is watching the movement of spreads between two different months. This type of analysis is considerably easier than tracking the varied groups in the stock market because the demarcations of groupings in the stock market are more subjective and there are more details to learn about individual companies. In the futures market, if you decide to track the movements of the soybean contract you need only specialize in soybeans. You don't have to specialize in a different underlying futures.

Tracking groups of commodities is more interesting, and more difficult. To track the metals complex, for example, you will have to know about the price movements of the individual commodities such as silver, gold, palladium, and platinum, and how they relate to the others. Tracking the strength of silver can be informative if the price of gold does not follow silver, but the analysis has to be more detailed and in-depth. The volatility due to the low margin requirements makes the futures industry less forgiving of mistakes. If you acquire a position in a laggard stock that does not move up with the leader, you have ample time and opportunities to unload the position without damage to your equity. In the stock market, laggards cannot become leaders, because their price action is too sluggish. In the volatile futures markets, laggards can be leaders to the downside, so futures requires more study and intense monitoring of market activity.

Sympathetic movements in the futures markets exist, but rarely and only under conditions of great strength. Unless the market is a raging bull, the trader will find it difficult for all the commodities within that complex to move in concert.

Today's market leaders may not be the leaders tomorrow, so it would be foolish to trade the followers based on this "expected" action of current leaders in the future. If the leaders show signs of weakness, look at the immediate followers and see if the others will follow when they move upwards. The weakness that develops in the laggards is the first signal that the current move up is about over.

RULE 43

Trade the Active Stocks and Futures

One of the yardsticks I use to analyze market activity of a particular stock issue or futures contract is the volume. I prefer to trade issues that have consistent trading volume activity.

Professional money managers do not trade low volume issues with no liquidity, but they do put on long-term positions in these issues based on careful fundamental analysis. They are, in effect, buying a company to own it and become part of management. Berkshire Hathaway, a former textile manufacturer turned into an investment vehicle by Warner Buffet, started off by accumulating formidable interests in smaller, well-run companies. It was essentially the only player in these companies and could dictate how the stock was acquired and distributed. For trading purposes, these same money managers will go towards the more liquid issues.

In futures, the less active markets are havens for floor traders and dens of bad execution for public orders. If you have ever traded any illiquid issues, you will know that the skids on the price executions are horrible. After all, floor traders make a living on public order flow. Unless you have very good fundamental and bullish analysis of the thin markets, it is best not to trade them.

I prefer to trade in markets with quite a bit of volume activity because I can enter and exit positions with ease. Remember, when you buy a stock, you are adding to the demand for the stock, so the price will probably move up when you buy. On the other side of the coin, when you sell a stock, you are adding to supply, so the price will probably move down when you sell. In either case, you want the stock price to go up *after* you buy and down after you sell. You don't want the market to move away from you when you are actually executing the trade. In a broad, liquid market, prices are less likely to move away from you when you are executing the trade because of the huge amount of trading interests in that market. In illiquid markets, you can essentially *become* the market by buying or selling a few shares or contracts; in such cases you might possibly be chasing the market to execute your trade.

I also stick with the active markets because they are less vulnerable to unfair manipulation. Note that I said "unfair" manipulation. As an experienced trader I assume that there is manipulation in all markets. When an experienced trader finds market manipulation going on, he or she wants to trade on the side of the big vested players. Substantial profits can be made riding the coattails of a properly marketed issue or futures. It only makes sense that investors or speculators with vested interests in a particular market would want to do whatever they can to support their positions: buying more to support, telling influential friends about the good investment, hyping future prospects of the investments—all legal activities. When the big players are supporting an issue or otherwise making their presence known to analysts, profits are easier to accumulate. Most big players will trade only in well-capitalized markets with broad participation. They don't want to get caught holding the bag if their analysis is incorrect. It doesn't take much to monopolize an inactive market; once that happens, other big players won't trade the issue because they know that the last one in the market will be the last one out. You, as a small trader or investor, don't want to get trampled when these big players start a run for the exit doors while you're walking in.

Information is readily available in widely traded issues. Thinly traded issues are quoted only in the pink sheets and have only a handful of market makers to provide information. Cocoa futures have so little trading activity that you have to obtain special reports to find out anything about it. With less information, you have less to come up with for an informed decision; you will be trading and speculating on incomplete information. I like to control where I send my trading capital.

Unsuccessful traders emphasize only the first part of a trade, the part that involves accumulating information to decide what to do in the markets, and ignore the last part of a trade, the part that involves getting out of a trade. Even if you were to get into a thinly traded issue and see it appreciate substantially in value, you can't realize the profit unless someone buys the issue from you. In illiquid issues, potential buyers are few and far between. You might think that there is always a buyer of any issue, whether you are selling your position out at a profit or at a loss; unfortunately, every other public investor in that thin issue is thinking along the same lines. When public investors start to run out the door at the same time, the bid-ask spread for the issue starts to widen and eventually disappears altogether. Market makers will make a market as long as they can profit from it; they will be the first ones to protect their trading positions when push comes to shove. In thoroughly liquid markets with depth of participation, there is always a buyer at a price that is not a giveaway.

If you are cashing in on a profitable position, you can afford to give away a few dollars to get a closeout position. If you are cutting your losses, you want to try to sell at your entry price, but, failing that, you want to get as close as you can to the last price. It is difficult to cut your losses in illiquid markets.

Table 43–1 **Trading Liquidity: Futures. (From *Technical Analysis of Stocks and Commodities,* June 1989. Used with permission.)**

Commodity Futures	Exchange	% Margin	Effective % Margin	Contracts to Trade for Equal Dollar Profit	Relative Contract Liquidity
Eurodollar	IMM	0.4	7.4	5	 100
Standard & Poor's 500	CME	10.0	24.9	1	 62
U.S. Treasury Bonds	CBT	2.8	14.7	4	 58
Crude Oil	NYM	10.0	19.4	6	. . . .
Soybeans	CBT	4.2	7.7	3	. . . . . .
Silver	CMX	8.6	9.2	2	. . . . . .
Gold	CMX	5.2	17.5	5	. . . . .
Japanese Yen ¥	IMM	1.8	5.00	2	. . . . .
Sugar-World #11	CSCE	14.7	23.0	7	. . . .
Corn	CBT	4.5	9.7	10	. . . .
10-Year Treasury Notes	CBT	1.6	11.2	5	. . .
West German Mark DM	IMM	2.1	5.7	2	. . .
Gasoline, Unleaded	NYM	7.3	13.6	4	. . .
Swiss Franc	IMM	2.2	6.9	2	. . .
Coffee "C"	CSCE	11.0	10.2	1	. . .
Heating Oil #2	NYM	9.2	12.3	4	. . .
Cattle, Live	CME	2.8	10.1	8	. .
Soybean Meal	CBT	4.6	8.4	5	. .
Copper	CMX	13.6	23.6	3	.
Soybean Oil	CBT	4.5	8.8	9	.
Cotton #2	CTN	4.7	8.7	4	.
Wheat	CBT	4.1	11.1	8	.
British Pound (new) £	IMM	3.0	13.3	3	.
Pork Bellies	CME	7.3	4.3	3	.
Cocoa	CSCE	7.0	8.7	6	.
5-Year Treasury Notes	CBT	1.3	16.9	8	.
Canadian Dollar	IMM	0.8	4.8	4	.
Major Market Maxi Index	CBT	5.3	11.0	1	.
NYSE Composite Index	NYFE	4.7	12.1	2	.
U.S. Treasury Bills	IMM	0.4	8.1	6	.
Municipal Bonds	CBT	1.4	7.5	4	.
Hogs	CME	4.4	10.4	10	.
Platinum	NYM	6.1	18.3	7	.
Wheat	KC	3.7	9.1	7	.
Cattle, Feeder	CME	2.3	7.0	5	.
U.S. Dollar Index	CNT	2.5	8.7	4	
Orange Juice	CTN	6.1	12.3	5	
Wheat	MPLS	3.6	9.0	7	
Value Line Average	KC	3.7	10.6	1	
Lumber	CME	3.0	12.8	10	
CRB Futures Price Index	NYFE	2.9	16.9	3	

Table 43–1   (Continued)

Commodity Futures	Exchange	% Margin	Effective % Margin	Contracts to Trade for Equal Dollar Profit	Relative Contract Liquidity
Silver	CBT	6.0	6.6	11	
Rapeseed (U.S. $)	WPG	4.3	11.2	27	
Soybeans	MCE	3.8	9.4	19	

CBT   Chicago Board of Trade
CME   Chicago Mercantile Exchange
CMX   Commodity Exchange, New York
CSCE   Coffee, Sugar & Cocoa Exchange, New York
CTN   New York Cotton Exchange
IMM   International Monetary Market at CME, Chicago
KC   Kansas City Board of Trade
MCE   MidAmerica Commodity Exchange, Chicago
MPLS   Minneapolis Grain Exchange
NYFE   New York Futures Exchange (New York Stock Exchange)
NYM   New York Mercantile Exchange
WPG   Winnipeg Commodity Exchange

Margin source: REFCO, Inc.

This is a reference chart for speculators. It compares markets according to their per-contract potential for profit and how easily contracts can be bought or sold (i.e., trading liquidity). Each is a proportional measure and is meaningful only when compared to others in the same column.

The number in the "Contracts to Trade for Equal Dollar Profit" column shows how many contracts of one commodity must be traded to obtain the same potential return as another commodity. Contracts to Trade = (Tick $ value) × (3-year Maximum Price Excursion).

"Relative Contract Liquidity" places commodities in descending order according to how easily all of their contracts can be traded. Commodities at the top of the list are easiest to buy and sell; commodities at the bottom of the list are the most difficult. "Relative Contract Liquidity" is the number of contracts to trade times total open interest times a volume factor which is:

$$1 \text{ or } \exp\left(\frac{\ln (volume)}{\ln (5000)}\right) - 2$$

RULE 44

Avoid Discretionary Accounts and Partnership Trading Accounts

Trading is a one-person business. If you are trading through a brokerage company, you can take recommendations from your broker, but you must not allow him or her to control your buying and selling.

When you are learning about the markets you must rely on your broker for information. Eventually, you want to learn enough from your broker so that you can do your own market analysis and have the broker merely execute your trades.

If you are not inclined to manage your own funds, then you have to seek the services of a broker who knows about the markets and give him or her carte blanche with your trading account. If your broker wants you to open a discretionary account, don't do it. If you are eager to partake in market action but don't have the time to actually manage your own funds, find a professional money manager. Discretionary accounts eventually lead to mismanagement of funds. I would recommend using a discretionary account on two conditions. The first is that your account is the only one the broker is handling so that it can receive the broker's undivided attention. The second condition is that the broker is not dependent on the commissions generated from your account to earn a living. Is there a broker out there who can qualify on both counts?

Partnership accounts also do not do well, although they have a chance to succeed if the responsibilities of each partner are delegated explicitly beforehand. Only one partner makes the analysis; the other one makes the executions. Neither can be involved in both.

One of the problems with partnership accounts is the fact that one person in the partnership is responsible for the complete assets of the account. This works well when the profits accumulate, but when the losses start to mount up arguments and fault finding often begin. The markets are erratic, and even the most seasoned investment professional can hit a losing streak. When that happens, even the partner with the firmest conviction that his partner analyzing the markets can weather the losses will find doubts.

The management success of futures options pools and stock mutual funds is attributable to the fact that the stockholders of the funds never see the actual money managers. At the end of the quarter they receive an impersonal report to stockholders. If stockholders want to cash out, they just sell out their interests in the secondary market. There is no personal interaction between the people who put up the money and the people who manage it.

In discretionary accounts and partnership accounts there is an interaction of two or three different players. When conflicts arise between partners in everyday life, they can be dealt with in an extended time frame. If partners in a trading account argue over whether a trade should be executed or not, or whether a bad trade should be closed out with current losses or not, they have to reach a decision quickly. Sometimes there are a lot of emotions seething below the surface.

When floor traders have outtrades, it is an accepted practice to close the trade immediately and split the loss evenly between both parties. In rare instances of disagreement, there is a mechanism to arbitrate the loss. This procedure is not possible in partnership trading accounts. Since one of the partners can be said to have greater input in trade execution, the other one will not want to share the losses equally.

To avoid problems with the management of mutual assets, it is best to avoid discretionary and partnership accounts. Either learn to trade yourself or find the services of a full-time money manager.

RULE 45

Bear Markets Have No Supports and Bull Markets Have No Resistance

I have often wondered why the markets never really find support at assumed levels and never meet resistance at former distribution points. Newsletter writers and market analysts with major research departments would often predict future support or resistance levels in the market. About half the time the levels of price support or resistance would hold and the markets would reverse from those levels as if repelled by unseen, magnetic forces. The other half of the time the markets would trade around those levels and then go right through them.

Why were these analysts and newsletter writers half right and half wrong? They failed to understand the actions of the market. In bullish markets, price congestion is supportive. In bearish markets, however, price congestion is resistive. I have observed the markets intensely for the last seventeen years and have found that in bull markets, there are no resistance levels overhead. In bear markets, there are no supports on the downside. How can the average trader profit from this simple observation?

Once analysts define a bull market, the prices of that market will rise gradually. There is more buying than there is selling at previous levels. As participants buy all that the market can currently offer, the supply of the issue or market moves from the hands of sellers to the hands of buyers. Price has to go up.

When analysts look at such price action, they look to previous price levels and arrive at important price gauges traveled by the market in the past. The analyst will view any chart formations that happened in the past as possible price reversal points in the current market action. The implicit assumption in their analysis is that the markets are currently undergoing a reaction in the continuing primary trend.

In a bull market, prices rise continuously, setting new highs. At some point in the market's upward journey, it pauses, creating an increasing supply of stocks or futures for sale at higher levels. This is the market top, which can be charted through technical analysis. Many analysts are unable to recognize the market top, however, as it is occurring, unless they happen to be charting that particular stock or future. Prices now erode. If the analyst sees a previous price level in which prices found a formation when the markets were bullish, the analyst is incorrect in saying that prices will find support again at those levels. The market is no longer bullish. If it were, it would find support at the previous congestion areas. But it is now bearish, and all supports will give way to continued selling pressures. Hence, the statement that in bear markets you should not worry about support levels, but about resistance levels.

The situation is the same if the markets have been in a massive bear trend and are now becoming bullish. Previous levels of congestion in the bear market are no longer valid in this new bull market. When prices move from the lows, the analyst cannot accurately say that they will stop rising at previous levels of congestion. Yes, there might be some minor trading, but these previous levels of congestion at higher prices when the market was bearish cannot be viewed as critical reversal points in the new bull markets. Instead of looking to sell out longs accumulated at lower prices at these congestion levels, the successful trader must look to add more once the price congestion is taken out; that is, once prices trade above the range of the congestion.

The only caveat here is in defining a bull or a bear market. If the analyst observes market action to be bullish for a number of months, the markets are probably bullish, and all retracements will find support at lower prices. If the analyst incorrectly analyzes the markets as continuing to be bullish when they aren't, then all retracements will *not* find support at lower price levels.

This can be attributed to the lack or the abundance of resistances and supports, which give the trader clues as to whether the markets are bullish or bearish.

In the stock market crash of 1987, Robert Prechter's previous support levels did not hold. The Dow industrials crashed through these support levels swiftly. In August 1987, the market showed topping action already; proficient analysts were aware that the intermediate term bull market was aging rapidly. When the stock market did crash in October 1987, supports were not to be found anywhere, at any price.

Similarly, bull markets have no resistances. The soybean markets featured consecutive new highs in 1972 (see Figure 20–1). Any trader selling short was scrambling to cover those shorts at higher prices. Actually, the bull market had been developing for years. With decreasing supplies and increasing demand for soybeans, the market's previous highs did not stop the price from continuing up. Fundamental analysis pointed to higher prices; technical analysis pointed to breakout markets. Foolish traders sold the new highs, all the way up.

The gold market, Figure 20–2, and the silver market, Figure 20–3, also showed massive bull markets. The prices of both these metals were artificially controlled through government interventions for decades. Once the decision was made to let prices float freely with market forces, the prices moved to all time contract highs. Again, many professional traders shorted all the way up.

Trends are all-powerful and will overcome any and all obstacles in their paths, which is why support levels never hold in bear markets.

The selling pressure is so strong in bear markets that all buyers at previous support levels are easily satisfied. Resistance levels never hold in bull markets either. The pent-up buying demand is so great that any sellers at previous resistance levels will easily be sold out.

When traders look at bar charts and say that a retracement is in store and look to be buying at previous support levels, they must also acknowledge whether or not they are still in a bull market. If the previous support levels prevent price erosion in the selloff, then the markets are probably still bullish. If the supports don't hold, that could indicate that the markets might possibly be turning from bullish to bearish. Once it is determined that the markets have turned bearish, then it is critical to trade in the direction of the newly established trend.

RULE 46

The Smarter You Are,
the Longer It Takes

Elsewhere in this book I discuss the old trader's rule of three tens. This rule said that a trader spends the first ten years of his life learning the business and scalping, the second ten years making money, and the third ten years managing that money in order to make more money.

It took much longer to become a success in the trading profession than I thought it would. I remember asking my supervisor at the First National Bank about taking a year's leave of absence so that I could trade futures for my own account. My request was denied, but I left the bank anyway and started my trading career in 1974. It took much longer than a year to make my fortune.

As in every profession or human endeavor, there are shortcuts to superficial success in trading. Some brokers churn their client equity to become high commission producers. Some traders pocket orders on the exchange floors, and some firm traders front run on orders. These are not the ones I consider to be successful in the real sense of the word. As an intelligent person you try to understand the basics of any situation: you ask who, what, when, where, and why. Once you understand a situation, you can apply it to another situation sometime in the future. This is what learning is about.

The markets, because they are composed of so many infinite variables, raise many more who, what, when, where, and why questions. This can create more confusion than clarification, yet it does not deny the need to know about the markets. In order to forecast imminent price moves, we absorb as much information as we can. There is a danger, however, if we go to the extreme and learn more than is needed to trade the markets successfully.

I was up in the trading room of my clearing firm one Friday afternoon at the end of a tough week. I blurted out to a couple of traders nearby that I hadn't made any money that week because I was too smart for the game.

Can anyone be too smart for the trading game? The answer is yes. If you look at the markets in their simplest form, you realize that there are essentially only three actions you can perform: you buy it, you sell it, or you hold it. This is the beauty of the markets: There is no grey area where subjective judgment enters into the equation for correct analysis. Yet, the smarter ones among us are the first to look for the shadows.

If you buy something and it goes down, do you ask why or do you sell out? If you buy and it goes up, do you ask who is buying it or do you hang on? If you sell something short and it goes nowhere, do you wait for the next government report or do you close out your positions? The more intelligent you are, the more questions you have. We all think there is more to making money in the markets than buying, selling, and holding on.

I once taught a seminar on cyclic timing. A student in the seminar came up to me afterwards and told me that he had lost money trading on the Chicago Board Options

Exchange. His mentor, who specialized in time spreads, told the student to watch the spreads that oscillated between a positive value and a negative value. He told the student to buy the spread when it oscillated in one direction and sell it out when it oscillated the other way. The student lost money.

As I listened to him, I immediately saw the problem: The spread oscillated back and forth. All he had to do was put on the spread at one price, wait, and leg out of the spread when it went the opposite way. He could be making several hundred thousand dollars a year doing this.

The key to wealth in trading is simplicity. My student was trained to believe that in order to make a lot of money he had to work very hard. In reality, the principles you use to make money on a one-lot trade are the same principles you would use to make money on a hundred-lot trade. You don't have to work harder to take on bigger positions, just more intelligently. And the more intelligently you work, the easier it becomes to make money.

There is an inherent irony to success in the trading business: When you really start to make money, it becomes boring because only certain trading strategies and styles work in the market. Once you find a way to make money consistently, you cannot attempt to optimize your strategy. The more you optimize a trading strategy, the more market-specific it becomes. When the markets change, you will be stranded with a fully optimized strategy that is now looking for a market condition under which it can be traded successfully. When successful trading becomes boring, it becomes difficult to continue making money.

I've grouped together a few trading ideas to keep in mind, even after you have learned all you can about the markets.

1. If you have a game plan, stick with it.

2. If you want to trade in a bull market, always buy. Don't ever sell a bull market to get a position in it. Wait until the market reacts to get to a lower buying level.

3. If your mind is wandering all the time, watch a few more markets to keep busy. Bored minds open up closed wallets.

4. Develop outside activities. Read books, exercise often, and do things that can take your mind off of trading.

5. Isolate yourself from others who trade with their opinions because you don't want their opinions to become your own.

6. Don't tamper with your positions once they show profits.

7. Keep the winners and figure out ways to get rid of the losers.

If worse comes to worse and your mind is wandering all over the place getting you into losing trading situations, think about this: When you get older and your mind finally starts to slow down, you'll become a successful trader.

RULE 47

It Is Harder To Get out of a Trade Than To Get into One

Over the years of instructions to novice traders I have always heard the complaint that they can get into a trade correctly, but they can never get out of a trade correctly. When these novice traders become traders with average skills, the complaints lessen but still persist.

When average traders become superior traders, they complain about bad fills or about missing the sell or buy signals, but they never complain about not being able to get out of the markets correctly.

After thorough analysis, I determined why novice traders complain about not being able to get *out* of a trade correctly, regardless of it being a winner or loser, but seldom complain about getting *into* a trade correctly. The reason is that there are more opportunities to get into a trade than to get out of one, regardless of whether the trade was successful or not.

The tools needed to make a decision to enter into a trade are completely different from those needed to exit trades. Deciding whether or not to enter a trade involves making a probability analysis. A skilled trader analyzes a situation for its profit and loss potential before deciding whether or not to enter a trade. Because the trader is using these entry tools on a trade that doesn't yet exist, the trader uses his or her total knowledge of the market to analyze many different situations for opportunities. In the course of a trading week, there may be about 15 or 20 such opportunities passing by an intermediate-term trader.

Once the trader enters a trade, he or she no longer has 15 or 20 profit opportunities to consider. The trader now has only one position to manage. However, some traders mistakenly apply the many technical techniques to analyzing exit points of a single trade that they put on. *They are trying to maintain an opportunistic approach to the management of the trade.*

A good trader understands this distinction—the analysis of opportunities before the trade versus the management of the one trade after the trade is entered into. A superior trader knows how to manage that one trade for maximum profit.

There is only one way to manage a trade: If it shows a profit, let it run; if it shows a loss, find an exit point to limit the losses. The successful trader uses many techniques to enter a trade but uses only loss limitation techniques to exit a losing trade. The unsuccessful trader uses many techniques to enter a trade and uses many of the same techniques to remove him- or herself from winning trades! For instance, a trader might sell out at a small profit, having sold the high, only to find out later that the market continued to move in the direction of the previous trade. The trader could have made a larger profit had he not used entry techniques to exit the trade.

R U L E 4 8

Don't Talk About What You're Doing in the Markets

If you want to discuss your trades, do so only after they are closed out and you have taken your profits or losses, but never before. I learned this lesson in 1974 from a trader named Harold Goodman at the Chicago Open Board of Trade.

In 1974, the young turks in the minipits were traders who eventually went over to the major exchanges and established fame and further fortune: Richard Dennis, Tommy Willis, Jack Savage, and David Ware. Richard Dennis eventually became one of the biggest traders at the Chicago Board of Trade. He recently retired from managing money after making more than $200 million for his own trading account. Tommy Willis eventually found a partner and managed money. He still trades actively. David Ware made more than a million dollars in a year in which a million dollars was still considered money. He invested his money in California real estate in the 1970s.

These traders had one thing in common when it came to trading: They all relied on Harold Goodman for advice and expertise. Harold wrote a weekly newsletter for a company that was then known as Greene & Collins. Collins later took his operation to the Chicago Board of Trade and is now associated with Les Rosenthal in the firm of Rosenthal-Collins. Harold wrote one of the best newsletters in the industry. He had one of the sharpest trading minds that I ever encountered. While the young turks were learning the business, Harold was going about doing his: trading the primary trends. The Open Board of Trade traded job-lot-sized contracts of the primary markets, grains, meats, currencies, and options. The size of the contracts traded has no bearing on the trends of the markets. As long as Harold could buy all he wanted in bull markets and sell all he wanted in bear markets, he was happy and extremely profitable.

One day I was in the wheat minipit at the market close and the traders were evening up their positions. Harold walked into the pit, and Willis, Dennis, and Ware immediately began offering wheat and soybeans to him. Harold pulled out a bunch of trading cards and started carding down the offers. I later found out that he took everything the young turks sold. The next morning wheat opened lower. Soybeans opened unchanged to slightly higher. Corn opened steady and traded lower. Harold was at his trading desk on the floor watching the grains open. As the day progressed, the wheat stopped selling off, then firmed up, and then moved above the settlement price. Towards the end of the day, wheat, soybeans, and corn closed limit up. Ten minutes before the minimarkets closed, Harold walked into the pits and made offers to buy more corn and soybeans. He was one of those traders who knew the main trend of the markets he was trading and added to those positions. He had a conviction in the direction of the markets and he followed it religiously.

He knew what he was doing, and because he was the biggest trader at the Open Board, he served as an out for the smaller traders. If Willis and Dennis couldn't unload their inventory or cover their shorts before the markets closed, they would find Harold willing to take the other side. He would bail them out of bad positions.

An episode involving one of Harold's orders illustrated how he dealt with the people on the trading floor. Harold was long silver contracts, and silver prices were making new highs daily. He took a vacation in Hawaii and called his clearing firm from there to inquire about his positions. The telephone connection was very bad; a second and third connection showed no improvement. Before hanging up, Harold told the clerk to buy 1,000 silver contracts. Afterwards, it occurred to the clerk that he didn't know whether Harold meant to buy 1,000 contracts of Open Board silver, which traded in 1,000 ounces per contract, or 1,000 Chicago Board of Trade silver, which traded in 5,000 ounces per contract. The order was either for 1 million ounces of silver or for 5 million ounces. The clerk attempted to reach Harold in Hawaii, but he was nowhere to be found. To be safer than sorrier, the clerk executed the order for 1 million ounces of silver. Silver went up and the clerk wondered whether the order had been for 5 million.

Harold came back from Hawaii and checked his purchase and sale statements. He had wanted to buy 5 million ounces of silver. The clerk was in trouble—very expensive trouble. Silver prices had climbed 40 cents an ounce since the 1 million ounces were purchased. The clerk could find himself having to come up with the 4 million ounces of appreciated silver, totaling $1.6 million.

When the clerk told Harold the mistake, do you know what Harold did? He patted the clerk on the back and told him not to make such a mistake again, bad connection or no bad connection. He turned around and gave the same clerk an order to buy the 4 million ounces of silver that he didn't buy 40 cents lower. Harold was that type of trader. He knew the weaknesses and strengths of people and worked around them. He was a loner who had learned to rely only on himself. As such, he was harsher on himself than on others.

I learned many trading lessons from Harold, but one of the most memorable is from years ago. I am extremely fond of repeating one particular lesson to young traders—never talking about trades while I have them on.

Soybeans were strong one day, so I bought a few contracts. The prices whipped around the whole day and made me extremely nervous. After the close, I went over to the broadtape and looked for stories dealing with soybeans. The cash prices from the Midwest showed improvement. Export demand was good. Supplies were being drawn down. An extremely bullish scenario. Yet rumors swirled through the pit about a higher than expected production report due out the next day. The rumors had me on edge.

I walked over to Harold's desk on the trading floor. He was writing his weekly marketletter. I had spoken a few words to Harold in the months that I was at the exchange, but he didn't really know me. He looked up and asked me what I wanted.

I screwed up enough courage to ask him what was really on my mind. I wanted to find out what his position in soybeans was, whether he was long or short. If he was long I would agree with him. If he were short I would try to persuade him to think bullishly. I didn't ask him what his total position was. I asked him if he was long. The way I phrased my question I hoped he would take the cue that I was also long. If he said that he was long millions of bean contracts and that he wanted to buy more tomorrow morning, I would feel reassured. Instead, he threw down his pen, looked me in the eyes, and yelled out, "It's none of your goddamn business!" He folded his hands behind his head, leaned back on his chair and yelled again, "What business is it of yours to know what my position is?"

He must have felt my shock and embarrassment, for he softened his tone a little and said, "I have a position in beans and it's a big position. If you know my position, what can you do to help it? And if you don't know my position, what can you do to hurt it?

"If I tell you my position, which might be the opposite of your position, are you going to argue with me that you are right and I am wrong? Imagine if you can convince me that I am wrong. Are you going to be here tomorrow to tell me what to do with my position?

"If your position is the same as mine, are you going to give me some of your profits, or am I supposed to give you some of mine? Your knowing my position won't do a damn bit of good for it. In fact, your knowing will even distract me from maintaining an even keel in this play. Okay, Bill?"

At the time, the shock of being corrected by Harold prevented me from absorbing the impact of his words. Over the years I thought about what he said and it started to make sense. I learned from many hard knocks to keep my mouth shut about my positions. I had a tendency to be swayed by others' comments and opinions. If someone could come up with a better argument and analysis than I had, I was more than willing to reverse my positions on the next morning's opening bell. I learned that if I did that, I wouldn't have a game plan and I wouldn't know what to do afterwards. If I stuck with my own analysis, in the worst possible scenario I would at least have a feel of what to do. If I followed others' analyses, I had to rely on them.

Friends no longer ask me about my positions. When others offer to tell me about their positions, I nod and walk away. If they persist, I change the subject. I don't want to tell others about my positions and I don't want to know about theirs.

R U L E 4 9

When Time Is up, Markets Must Reverse

One aspect of market analysis is time cycle analysis. Almost everyone in the markets looks at only one aspect of the markets, price activity. Little thought is given to time and its respective cycles. Yet the factor of time in market forecasting is the most critical component of market analysis. It is more important than price or volume analysis.

When you read the stock or futures quotes in the *Wall Street Journal,* the first piece of information that you look for is the closing prices of the markets in which you have interests. With price activity you assess whether or not you made money from the previous reporting period, which in this case is the previous day. In reading the weekly issue of *Barron's,* you would be comparing the weekly closing prices with the previous week's. In either case, you would be comparing price changes.

A comparison of two closing periods' prices is based on the assumption that those prices are representative of the daily or weekly activity of those markets. Although this is generally correct, at times the assumption is not accurate and may get the trader into analytical trouble. The trader who strictly uses price activity will be making wrong conclusions about market behavior at those particular times.

An example of where an incorrect conclusion based solely on price activity can be made is found in trading range markets. Once several tops and bottoms are defined at the same approximate price levels, the trader uses the upper and lower prices, respectively, as general sell and buy levels. But professional traders know that trading markets breed trending markets. Eventually, these upper and lower price limits will give way to strongly defined trends. The last trade at the upper price limit might be followed by a strong move against the trader who is unfortunate enough to have sold at the upside breakout. Conversely, the last trade at the lower price limit might be followed by a massive price collapse if he is unfortunate enough to have bought the lower range.

To compound the trader's difficulty in determining whether he is selling the rally or buying the break, as opposed to selling at the bottom of an uptrend or buying the top of the collapse, price behavior gives false signals. For example, if the trader is using price breakouts as an indicator to institute positions in the direction of the breakouts, he will be presented with quite a few of these false breakouts.

In trading range markets, the trader, who believes he might be buying into an upside breakout when the price activity edges up several fractions above the previous highs of the range, might be long at the top because prices start downwards again. If this unfortunate trader wishes to continue to do this, he could do what old-time traders used to do to mitigate the problem: bludgeon the market to death. The old-timers would merely get rid of their longs and take their losses. They would consistently do this and take their losses every time the market failed to follow through on upside breakouts. They were never able to make money in trading range markets because instead of waiting to sell the upper prices and buy the lower prices, they were prone to buying the upside breakouts and selling the downside breakdowns.

I now have presented two types of trading strategies based on the use of price as markers: sell the tops or buy the bottoms in trading range markets; buy the upside breakouts or sell the downside collapses in anticipation of the development of trending markets.

Market plays executed with finesse appeal to me. The thought of bludgeoning the market to death makes me cringe. I would rather think myself to wealth instead of sweating to wealth.

In addition to viewing market action based on price, the trader must view the action from the perspectives of time and volume. Volume is too difficult a matter to deal with in this chapter, but I can elaborate on the aspect of time.

Time is another component of market forecasting. The unique feature time has, which volume and price don't have, is that it can be forecasted well in advance of present situations in the markets. You cannot forecast price and volume activity in advance.

In the example earlier in this chapter, where the trader is strictly using price indicators, the use of time indicators, or time cycles, would reduce the number of potentially false price signals. Time cycle analysis will offer you insight on how to make sure that moves into the upper range of a sell area or into the lower range of a buy area in a trading range market should warrant respective sell or buy actions.

After a trading range is defined by several upper and lower price boundaries, you can discover the existence of several different time cycles oscillating from high to low. If the current low price of the market also coincides with a time cycle trough, then buying action is warranted.

249

Buying is warranted in two cases. In the first case, the price is at the low of the price range. If you are a trading range speculator, purchasing the market would insure that you will profit by at least the amount price moves to the upper area of your trading range. In the second case, if no time cycle peaks are imminent, you can assume, with a high degree of probability, that when price reaches the upper trading range it will follow through on an upside breakout. In this second scenario, breakouts to the upside are more believable than in a situation where a time cycle peak coincided with a price move to the upper end of the trading range.

By looking at time cycles, we have added another dimension to market analysis. In our one dimensional viewpoint we looked at market action as merely price activity. We have now narrowed these critical price activity points into more valid order execution points through the addition of time cycles.

From my own experience, I believe time cycles take precedence over price activity in respect to market action forecasting. However, price activity takes precedence in respect to actual market trading. Time cycles take precedence when we are attempting to forecast market activity because of the obvious fact that time can be forecast in advance.

Time, as measured by humans, is the tracking of motion in space. For example, the use of a clock implies that motion is tracked circularly by three guides: the second, minute, and hour hands. From these basic guides, we can project linear cycles into the future. We can forecast that 24 hours from now will mark the spatial movement of another complete revolution of the earth on its own axis. We can forecast that 365 days from now the earth will complete one revolution around the sun. This goes on and on, using all the planetary motions.

As we can predict the motion of the planets, we can predict where our clock hands will be for any future time.

The strength of time cycles—they can be forecasted in advance—is countered by their weakness—there is no absolute adherence of market events to these precise cycles.

Traders delude themselves into believing that the precision of time cycles will be extended to precise price analysis. This is not yet possible. Yet, here is a blessing in disguise: If adherence of unpredictable price activity to predictable time cycles must be attempted, what other way exists than to try to integrate the two into a paradigm of market analysis?

To finalize this chapter, price activity takes precedence over time cycles as far as we frail humans are concerned. This is obvious because the value of your trading equity is defined by the amount of money you have in your account. Your positions in the markets are tied to price activity; your position is marked to the last market price, not the last time cycle peak or bottom. Yet, within this idea, price is also enslaved to time: When the closing bell rings, price freezes. Time continues on, while price is in suspended animation. Price will only change when it is time for the markets to reopen for trading.

As powerful as time is, it is also enslaved to price because the price of whatever markets are tracked is most important to success or failure in trading.

251

RULE 50

Control What You Can,
Manage What You Cannot

Traders who are unsuccessful in the markets do not understand their roles in relation to the market's perspective. Traders are small players in the context of the market's overall existence. Not only must they recognize this fact, they also must never think otherwise. No matter how much money the trader has to invest in the market, the market is the market.

Which aspects of investing and speculating does the trader control, and what does he have no say in? When does a trader switch from a leader to a follower? How important is it to a trader's success to know when and how to follow or lead?

The following are items that the trader can, and must, control:

- The amount of money put into the markets.
- The number of markets to follow.
- When to enter a trade.

- How to enter a trade.
- When to exit a trade.
- How to exit a trade.
- How to spend one's time.

There is no need to determine probabilities that a trader has a certain amount of capital to put into the market or when he enters into a trade. There is 100% certainty that the trader can put X amount into the markets and can put in a trade on, say, Monday morning 5 minutes and 30 seconds after the first trade in soybeans.

The following are items over which the trader has absolutely no control:

- The direction markets will move.
- The duration of the markets' movements.

Failure to recognize these aspects of the markets early will result in failure at trading. And the irony is that a trader will end his career without knowing why he failed.

Problems occur, and failures materialize, when the trader starts to believe that the power which comes with controlling what he can control can be exercised in situations over which he has no control. The market moves whenever and however it wants to. If the trader believes he can dictate to the market when and how he wants it to move, surprises occur.

The mere act of buying or selling a futures contract or a stock implies that you want that particular instrument to move up or down. When you buy, you want it to go up. When you sell, you want it to go down. What is mistaken is the fact that when you buy and it goes up, you are really buying something that is already strong. Your buying does not make it stronger.

One act of buying or selling has no extended impact on the market. Except for the extreme case where individual buying or selling can actually move the market when others follow in concerted action, it is impossible to buy and have the market go up immediately afterward, or sell and have the market go down immediately.

You were there at the right time and right place. In the worst scenario of timing, you merely followed the market, and in the best scenario, you anticipated the market's move. In either case, you had no control over it. If you weren't the one who bought the lows or sold the highs, it would have been some other person. And if the market didn't move after you bought or sold, it would have eventually, independent of your actions.

A friend related an incident many years ago which illustrates the subject of this chapter explicitly. Ralph Peters was Chairman of the Chicago Board of Trade around the time I became a member of the exchange. (He passed away recently at the age of 56. His estate was valued at between $300 and $500 million. Once these numbers are reached, who cares if you give or take a couple hundred million?)

A broker friend had been following the recently initiated trading in S & P 500 futures at the Chicago Mercantile Exchange. My friend's eclectic and highly mathematical calculations determined that a critical number would be a strong resistance point. He got his clients short just below the critical point and placed stop buy orders several ticks above the critical point to protect his clients' short positions.

The market was bullish, continually making higher highs and higher lows. This one particular day's trading activity showed strength. It reached up just shy of the critical number and sold off. It reached up again to a fraction higher than before and then sold off. The second sell-off stopped short of the first reaction's low. A higher low pattern formed. For the third rally it stalled right at the critical number. There was obvious interest at that critical number because prices churned around at that number for minutes, which seemed like hours.

Boom. The critical number did not hold. In rapid succession trades went across a tick above the critical number, then another quote a tick higher.

Only after the market made new highs by four ticks did it exhaust itself and back off. As the selling came back into the market, prices dropped below the critical number. My friend, astonished at the market's drive to reach his stops, cursed his bad luck.

My friend waited for the fills on his stop buy orders. He waited. Still no fills. He wondered whether or not the clerks misplaced his orders and perhaps he luckily had not been stopped out of his initial shorts. He called down to the floor a half hour after the market closed and requested fills.

The clerk reported that the fills on the stops were cancelled and described the scene on the floor several hours earlier when the market pushed past the critical number. Ralph Peters had also been watching that critical number from his office. However, he watched it from the perspective of a person wanting to challenge it, not of a person following the markets. The first time the market moved close to the critical number, he had discretely entered buy orders. The second time it got up fractionally higher he had also been a discrete buyer. But the third time he tested his will against the market's omnipotence. He entered an order to buy 1,000 contracts right at the critical number, the first time in S & P futures contract trading history that such an order was entered.

The locals panicked and bought everything they could. They pushed the market higher and caught all the stops several ticks above the critical number.

After the 1,000 contract had been filled, along with a bunch of others around that price level, other brokers at the other side of the trading pit screamed that they had thousands of sell orders—below the critical number. There was no way that any orders could trade above these resting orders, given the supply of contracts offered for sale.

The pit cancelled the highest tick, then the next highest, all the way down to the critical number. Prices on market orders were lowered to adjust the fills to reflect the new lower day's high. Limit stop buy orders above the adjusted high were now cancelled. My friend's orders to stop buy were never filled.

The market had a critical number to resist any further up move for the time being. One person tried to bull the market into submission and failed. This incident illustrates the fact that there are things that a trader can control and things that he cannot. There are things that are strictly in the province of the market and can never be broached even by one of the best speculators.

The day's high eventually gave way to further up-moves, but only when the market was ready to let it do so. And not before. In the case of this trader, the losses he sustained were controlled. For the price of several hundred thousand dollars, he found out what he could not control. He could not control the market. This lesson was cheap compared to the money that he was eventually able to accumulate.

As far as your own trading is concerned, make sure that if and when you get a ridiculous scheme to move the markets that the money you have at stake is what you can afford to lose. If not, save yourself the aggravation and look for another career.

CONCLUSION

The 360-Degree Wheel
Theory

Market knowledge is an accumulation of many experiences. The rules that I have gathered in this book have been developed by expert market minds. I have merely applied them to current markets.

The 50 or so rules that I have elaborated on in this book became known to me in 1971, the first year I traded the markets. Over the last 18 years I have journeyed into stocks, options, and futures markets and learned as much about the ramifications of these rules as I could without an instructor at my side. Around the ninth year of my journey into market knowledge some of the rules that I learned in the first year started to make sense.

A case in point is the old saying that the only way to make a small fortune in the commodity markets is to start with a large fortune. When I heard this saying in the first year of my career, my first reaction was to laugh at the cynicism inherent in the statement. I thought the rule stated that if I wanted to make $500,000 in the markets, I had to start with $1 million. By the time I finished trading and lost half of my startup capital, I would have wound up with the other half, that is, the small fortune.

Years of trading experience have taught me to reinterpret that statement not as cynicism, but as common sense money management. Embedded in the statement is the key to market survival: In order to make a better than average return, you need a large enough sum to trade and manage. To make $500,000 all you need is a 50 percent annualized return on a larger fortune, the $1 million. The original statement means to say that you cannot make $500,000 yearly by starting with $25,000. The original sum has to be larger.

If I only knew then what I know now . . .

Another rule that I eventually interpreted correctly is Rule 28 in this book: Always buy new highs. I wrote that I always lost money when I did this. I had to sell out the longs I bought at new high prices after the markets retraced. I eventually found out that the action of buying the high was part of a more complete trading strategy. You have to be long at lower prices before you can buy new highs with safety. Buying new highs in itself is foolish and can only guarantee that prices will retrace and hand you losses. However, if buying new highs is adding to long positions accumulated at lower prices, then you cannot help but make money from the total position in bullish markets. This rule made trading sense when I saw it from a larger perspective.

Perspective is what makes traders successful. The ability to see these single sentence rules in the larger perspective of a trading paradigm helps traders succeed in markets.

The 360-degree wheel theory breaks down a trader's career into three time periods. In the first ten years you learn the rules and see how they play out in the markets. You don't know their exact meaning, but you do know that they sometimes work. At other times they fail miserably, like the rule of buying new highs. During this stage your thought is to buy new highs.

As the second decade starts, you see the same rules from a slightly different perspective, one with more depth. Your rule to buy new highs now reads like this: Buy new highs, but use your experience to isolate market events with discrimination. Before reaching this stage of the learning curve, you applied the rule indiscriminately.

Finally, on the third trip around the wheel, you are wiser still in your knowledge of the markets. The rules have remained the same, but the number of exceptions is greater. Now you can discard the application of certain rules under certain market conditions, whereas before, you applied the rules all the time, with a careful eye to the exceptions. At this point you are truly a wise speculator.

If you are fortunate and persistent enough to make it past the first revolution of knowledge, you will make money in the markets. If you are good enough to make it past the second revolution of experience, you can impart your knowledge to others. And if you are wise enough to make it past the third revolution of wisdom, you will indeed retire a very wealthy person.

INDEX